Singapore MATH PRACTICE

LEVEL 4A

6

App... Students in

Frank Schaffer

An imprint of Carson-Dellosa Publishing LLC

Greensboro, North Carolina

Copyright © 2009 Singapore Asian Publications (S) Pte. Ltd.

Frank Schaffer
An imprint of Carson-Dellosa Publishing LLC
PO Box 35665
Greensboro, NC 27425 USA

Printed in the USA • All rights reserved.
4 5 6 7 GLO 13 12 11 10

ISBN 978-0-7682-3995-9
245107784

INTRODUCTION TO SINGAPORE MATH

Welcome to Singapore Math! The math curriculum in Singapore has been recognized worldwide for its excellence in producing students highly skilled in mathematics. Students in Singapore have ranked at the top in the world in mathematics on the *Trends in International Mathematics and Science Study* (TIMSS) in 1993, 1995, 2003, and 2008. Because of this, Singapore Math has gained in interest and popularity in the United States.

Singapore Math curriculum aims to help students develop the necessary math concepts and process skills for everyday life and to provide students with the ability to formulate, apply, and solve problems. Mathematics in the Singapore Primary (Elementary) Curriculum cover fewer topics but in greater depth. Key math concepts are introduced and built-on to reinforce various mathematical ideas and thinking. Students in Singapore are typically one grade level ahead of students in the United States.

The following pages provide examples of the various math problem types and skill sets taught in Singapore.

At an elementary level, some simple mathematical skills can help students understand mathematical principles. These skills are the counting-on, counting-back, and crossing-out methods. Note that these methods are most useful when the numbers are small.

1. The Counting-On Method

Used for addition of two numbers. Count on in 1s with the help of a picture or number line.

$$7 + 4 = \mathbf{11}$$

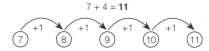

2. The Counting-Back Method

Used for subtraction of two numbers. Count back in 1s with the help of a picture or number line.

$$16 - 3 = \mathbf{13}$$

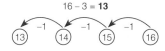

3. The Crossing-Out Method

Used for subtraction of two numbers. Cross out the number of items to be taken away. Count the remaining ones to find the answer.

$$20 - 12 = \mathbf{8}$$

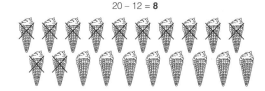

A **number bond** shows the relationship in a simple addition or subtraction problem. The number bond is based on the concept "part-part-whole." This concept is useful in teaching simple addition and subtraction to young children.

To find a whole, students must add the two parts.
To find a part, students must subtract the other part from the whole.

The different types of number bonds are illustrated below.

1. Number Bond (single digits)

$$3 \text{ (part)} + 6 \text{ (part)} = \mathbf{9} \text{ (whole)}$$
$$9 \text{ (whole)} - 3 \text{ (part)} = \mathbf{6} \text{ (part)}$$
$$9 \text{ (whole)} - 6 \text{ (part)} = \mathbf{3} \text{ (part)}$$

2. Addition Number Bond (single digits)

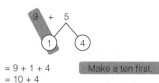

$$= 9 + 1 + 4$$
$$= 10 + 4$$
$$= \mathbf{14}$$

Make a ten first

3. Addition Number Bond (double and single digits)

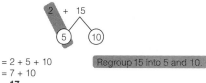

$$= 2 + 5 + 10$$
$$= 7 + 10$$
$$= \mathbf{17}$$

Regroup 15 into 5 and 10.

4. Subtraction Number Bond (double and single digits)

$$10 - 7 = 3$$
$$3 + 2 = \mathbf{5}$$

5. Subtraction Number Bond (double digits)

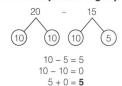

$$10 - 5 = 5$$
$$10 - 10 = 0$$
$$5 + 0 = \mathbf{5}$$

Students should understand that multiplication is repeated addition and that division is the grouping of all items into equal sets.

1. Repeated Addition (Multiplication)

Mackenzie eats 2 rolls a day. How many rolls does she eat in 5 days?

$$2 + 2 + 2 + 2 + 2 = 10$$
$$5 \times 2 = 10$$

She eats **10** rolls in 5 days.

2. The Grouping Method (Division)

Mrs. Lee makes 14 sandwiches. She gives all the sandwiches equally to 7 friends. How many sandwiches does each friend receive?

$$14 \div 7 = 2$$

Each friend receives **2** sandwiches.

One of the basic but essential math skills students should acquire is to perform the 4 operations of whole numbers and fractions. Each of these methods is illustrated below.

1. The Adding-Without-Regrouping Method

H	T	O	
3	2	1	O: Ones
+ 5	6	8	T: Tens
8	**8**	**9**	H: Hundreds

Since no regrouping is required, add the digits in each place value accordingly.

2. The Adding-by-Regrouping Method

H	T	O	
¹4	9	2	O: Ones
+ 1	5	3	T: Tens
6	**4**	**5**	H: Hundreds

In this example, regroup 14 tens into 1 hundred 4 tens.

3

Singapore Math Practice Level 5A

3. The Adding-by-Regrouping-Twice Method

$$
\begin{array}{ccc}
H & T & O \\
{}^1 2 & {}^1 8 & 6 \\
+\ 3 & 6 & 5 \\
\hline
6 & 5 & 1 \\
\end{array}
$$

O: Ones
T: Tens
H: Hundreds

Regroup twice in this example.
First, regroup 11 ones into 1 ten 1 one.
Second, regroup 15 tens into 1 hundred 5 tens.

4. The Subtracting-Without-Regrouping Method

$$
\begin{array}{ccc}
H & T & O \\
7 & 3 & 9 \\
-\ 3 & 2 & 5 \\
\hline
4 & 1 & 4 \\
\end{array}
$$

O: Ones
T: Tens
H: Hundreds

Since no regrouping is required, subtract the digits in each place value accordingly.

5. The Subtracting-by-Regrouping Method

$$
\begin{array}{ccc}
H & T & O \\
5 & {}^7 \cancel{8} & {}^{11} \cancel{1} \\
-\ 2 & 4 & 7 \\
\hline
3 & 3 & 4 \\
\end{array}
$$

O: Ones
T: Tens
H: Hundreds

In this example, students cannot subtract 7 ones from 1 one. So, regroup the tens and ones. Regroup 8 tens 1 one into 7 tens 11 ones.

6. The Subtracting-by-Regrouping-Twice Method

$$
\begin{array}{ccc}
H & T & O \\
{}^7 \cancel{8} & {}^9 \cancel{0} & {}^{10} \cancel{0} \\
-\ 5 & 9 & 3 \\
\hline
2 & 0 & 7 \\
\end{array}
$$

O: Ones
T: Tens
H: Hundreds

In this example, students cannot subtract 3 ones from 0 ones and 9 tens from 0 tens. So, regroup the hundreds, tens, and ones. Regroup 8 hundreds into 7 hundreds 9 tens 10 ones.

7. The Multiplying-Without-Regrouping Method

$$
\begin{array}{cc}
T & O \\
2 & 4 \\
\times & 2 \\
\hline
4 & 8 \\
\end{array}
$$

O: Ones
T: Tens

Since no regrouping is required, multiply the digit in each place value by the multiplier accordingly.

8. The Multiplying-With-Regrouping Method

$$
\begin{array}{ccc}
H & T & O \\
{}^1 3 & {}^2 4 & 9 \\
\times & & 3 \\
\hline
1, 0 & 4 & 7 \\
\end{array}
$$

O: Ones
T: Tens
H: Hundreds

In this example, regroup 27 ones into 2 tens 7 ones, and 14 tens into 1 hundred 4 tens.

9. The Dividing-Without-Regrouping Method

$$
\begin{array}{r}
241 \\
2\,\overline{)\,482\,} \\
-4 \\
\hline
8 \\
-8 \\
\hline
2 \\
-2 \\
\hline
0 \\
\end{array}
$$

Since no regrouping is required, divide the digit in each place value by the divisor accordingly.

10. The Dividing-With-Regrouping Method

$$
\begin{array}{r}
166 \\
5\,\overline{)\,830\,} \\
-5 \\
\hline
33 \\
-30 \\
\hline
30 \\
-30 \\
\hline
0 \\
\end{array}
$$

In this example, regroup 3 hundreds into 30 tens and add 3 tens to make 33 tens. Regroup 3 tens into 30 ones.

11. The Addition-of-Fractions Method

$$
\frac{1 \times 2}{6 \times 2} + \frac{1 \times 3}{4 \times 3} = \frac{2}{12} + \frac{3}{12} = \frac{5}{12}
$$

Always remember to make the denominators common before adding the fractions.

12. The Subtraction-of-Fractions Method

$$
\frac{1 \times 5}{2 \times 5} - \frac{1 \times 2}{5 \times 2} = \frac{5}{10} - \frac{2}{10} = \frac{3}{10}
$$

Always remembers to make the denominators common before subtracting the fractions.

13. The Multiplication-of-Fractions Method

$$
\frac{{}^1 \cancel{3}}{5} \times \frac{1}{\cancel{9}_{3}} = \frac{1}{15}
$$

When the numerator and the denominator have a common multiple, reduce them to their lowest fractions.

14. The Division-of-Fractions Method

$$
\frac{7}{9} \div \frac{1}{6} = \frac{7}{\cancel{9}_{3}} \times \frac{\cancel{6}^{2}}{1} = \frac{14}{3} = 4\frac{2}{3}
$$

When dividing fractions, first change the division sign (÷) to the multiplication sign (×). Then, switch the numerator and denominator of the fraction on the right hand side. Multiply the fractions in the usual way.

Model drawing is an effective strategy used to solve math word problems. It is a visual representation of the information in word problems using bar units. By drawing the models, students will know of the variables given in the problem, the variables to find, and even the methods used to solve the problem.

Drawing models is also a versatile strategy. It can be applied to simple word problems involving addition, subtraction, multiplication, and division. It can also be applied to word problems related to fractions, decimals, percentage, and ratio.

The use of models also trains students to think in an algebraic manner, which uses symbols for representation.

The different types of bar models used to solve word problems are illustrated below.

1. The model that involves addition

Melissa has 50 blue beads and 20 red beads. How many beads does she have altogether?

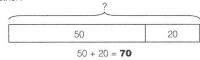

$$50 + 20 = \mathbf{70}$$

2. The model that involves subtraction

Ben and Andy have 90 toy cars. Andy has 60 toy cars. How many toy cars does Ben have?

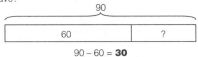

$$90 - 60 = \mathbf{30}$$

3. The model that involves comparison

Mr. Simons has 150 magazines and 110 books in his study. How many more magazines than books does he have?

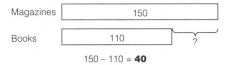

$$150 - 110 = \mathbf{40}$$

4. The model that involves two items with a difference

A pair of shoes costs $109. A leather bag costs $241 more than the pair of shoes. How much is the leather bag?

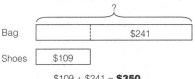

$$\$109 + \$241 = \mathbf{\$350}$$

5. The model that involves multiples

Mrs. Drew buys 12 apples. She buys 3 times as many oranges as apples. She also buys 3 times as many cherries as oranges. How many pieces of fruit does she buy altogether?

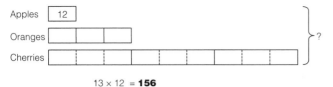

$$13 \times 12 = \mathbf{156}$$

6. The model that involves multiples and difference

There are 15 students in Class A. There are 5 more students in Class B than in Class A. There are 3 times as many students in Class C than in Class A. How many students are there altogether in the three classes?

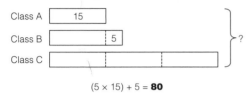

$$(5 \times 15) + 5 = \mathbf{80}$$

7. The model that involves creating a whole

Ellen, Giselle, and Brenda bake 111 muffins. Giselle bakes twice as many muffins as Brenda. Ellen bakes 9 fewer muffins than Giselle. How many muffins does Ellen bake?

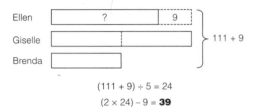

$$(111 + 9) \div 5 = 24$$
$$(2 \times 24) - 9 = \mathbf{39}$$

8. The model that involves sharing

There are 183 tennis balls in Basket A and 97 tennis balls in Basket B. How many tennis balls must be transferred from Basket A to Basket B so that both baskets contain the same number of tennis balls?

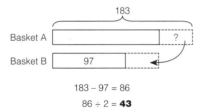

$$183 - 97 = 86$$
$$86 \div 2 = \mathbf{43}$$

9. The model that involves fractions

George had 355 marbles. He lost $\frac{1}{5}$ of the marbles and gave $\frac{1}{4}$ of the remaining marbles to his brother. How many marbles did he have left?

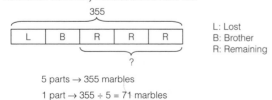

L: Lost
B: Brother
R: Remaining

5 parts → 355 marbles
1 part → 355 ÷ 5 = 71 marbles
3 parts → 3 × 71 = **213** marbles

10. The model that involves ratio

Aaron buys a tie and a belt. The prices of the tie and belt are in the ratio 2 : 5. If both items cost $539,

(a) what is the price of the tie?

(b) what is the price of the belt?

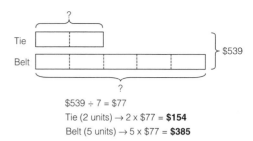

$$\$539 \div 7 = \$77$$
Tie (2 units) → 2 × $77 = **$154**
Belt (5 units) → 5 × $77 = **$385**

11. The model that involves comparison of fractions

Jack's height is $\frac{2}{3}$ of Leslie's height. Leslie's height is $\frac{3}{4}$ of Lindsay's height. If Lindsay is 160 cm tall, find Jack's height and Leslie's height.

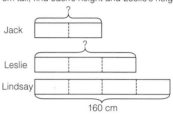

1 unit → 160 ÷ 4 = 40 cm
Leslie's height (3 units) → 3 × 40 = **120 cm**
Jack's height (2 units) → 2 × 40 = **80 cm**

Thinking skills and strategies are important in mathematical problem solving. These skills are applied when students think through the math problems to solve them. Below are some commonly used thinking skills and strategies applied in mathematical problem solving.

1. Comparing

Comparing is a form of thinking skill that students can apply to identify similarities and differences.

When comparing numbers, look carefully at each digit before deciding if a number is greater or less than the other. Students might also use a number line for comparison when there are more numbers.

Example:

3 is greater than 2 but smaller than 7.

2. Sequencing

A sequence shows the order of a series of numbers. *Sequencing* is a form of thinking skill that requires students to place numbers in a particular order. There are many terms in a sequence. The terms refer to the numbers in a sequence.

To place numbers in a correct order, students must first find a rule that generates the sequence. In a simple math sequence, students can either add or subtract to find the unknown terms in the sequence.

Example: Find the 7th term in the sequence below.

1,	4,	7,	10,	13,	16	?
1st term	2nd term	3rd term	4th term	5th term	6th term	7th term

Step 1: This sequence is in an increasing order.

Step 2: 4 – 1 = 3   7 – 4 = 3
The difference between two consecutive terms is 3.

Step 3: 16 + 3 = 19
The 7th term is **19**.

3. Visualization

Visualization is a problem solving strategy that can help students visualize a problem through the use of physical objects. Students will play a more active role in solving the problem by manipulating these objects.

The main advantage of using this strategy is the mobility of information in the process of solving the problem. When students make a wrong step in the process, they can retrace the step without erasing or canceling it.

The other advantage is that this strategy helps develop a better understanding of the problem or solution through visual objects or images. In this way, students will be better able to remember how to solve these types of problems.

Singapore Math Practice Level 5A

Some of the commonly used objects for this strategy are toothpicks, straws, cards, strings, water, sand, pencils, paper, and dice.

4. Look for a Pattern

This strategy requires the use of observational and analytical skills. Students have to observe the given data to find a pattern in order to solve the problem. Math word problems that involve the use of this strategy usually have repeated numbers or patterns.

Example: Find the sum of all the numbers from 1 to 100.

Step 1: Simplify the problem.
   Find the sum of 1, 2, 3, 4, 5, 6, 7, 8, 9, and 10.

Step 2: Look for a pattern.

$1 + 10 = 11$	$2 + 9 = 11$	$3 + 8 = 11$
$4 + 7 = 11$	$5 + 6 = 11$	

Step 3: Describe the pattern.
   When finding the sum of 1 to 10, add the first and last numbers to get a result of 11. Then, add the second and second last numbers to get the same result. The pattern continues until all the numbers from 1 to 10 are added. There will be 5 pairs of such results. Since each addition equals 11, the answer is then $5 \times 11 = 55$.

Step 4: Use the pattern to find the answer.
   Since there are 5 pairs in the sum of 1 to 10, there should be ($10 \times 5 = 50$ pairs) in the sum of 1 to 100.

   Note that the addition for each pair is not equal to 11 now. The addition for each pair is now ($1 + 100 = 101$).
   $$50 \times 101 = 5050$$
   The sum of all the numbers from 1 to 100 is **5,050**.

5. Working Backward

The strategy of working backward applies only to a specific type of math word problem. These word problems state the end result, and students are required to find the total number. In order to solve these word problems, students have to work backward by thinking through the correct sequence of events. The strategy of working backward allows students to use their logical reasoning and sequencing to find the answers.

Example: Sarah has a piece of ribbon. She cuts the ribbon into 4 equal parts. Each part is then cut into 3 smaller equal parts. If the length of each small part is 35 cm, how long is the piece of ribbon?
   $$3 \times 35 = 105 \text{ cm}$$
   $$4 \times 105 = 420 \text{ cm}$$
   The piece of ribbon is **420 cm**.

6. The Before-After Concept

The *Before-After* concept lists all the relevant data before and after an event. Students can then compare the differences and eventually solve the problems. Usually, the Before-After concept and the mathematical model go hand in hand to solve math word problems. Note that the Before-After concept can be applied only to a certain type of math word problem, which trains students to think sequentially.

Example: Kelly has 4 times as much money as Joey. After Kelly uses some money to buy a tennis racquet, and Joey uses $30 to buy a pair of pants, Kelly has twice as much money as Joey. If Joey has $98 in the beginning,
   (a) how much money does Kelly have in the end?
   (b) how much money does Kelly spend on the tennis racquet?

Before

Kelly

Joey $98

After

Kelly

Joey

   (a) $98 - $30 = $68
      $2 \times $68 = $136
      Kelly has **$136** in the end.
   (b) $4 \times $98 = $392
      $392 - $136 = $256
      Kelly spends **$256** on the tennis racquet.

7. Making Supposition

Making supposition is commonly known as "making an assumption." Students can use this strategy to solve certain types of math word problems. Making assumptions will eliminate some possibilities and simplifies the word problems by providing a boundary of values to work within.

Example: Mrs. Jackson bought 100 pieces of candy for all the students in her class. How many pieces of candy would each student receive if there were 25 students in her class?

In the above word problem, assume that each student received the same number of pieces. This eliminates the possibilities that some students would receive more than others due to good behaviour, better results, or any other reason.

8. Representation of Problem

In problem solving, students often use representations in the solutions to show their understanding of the problems. Using representations also allow students to understand the mathematical concepts and relationships as well as to manipulate the information presented in the problems. Examples of representations are diagrams and lists or tables.

Diagrams allow students to consolidate or organize the information given in the problems. By drawing a diagram, students can see the problem clearly and solve it effectively.

A list or table can help students organize information that is useful for analysis. After analyzing, students can then see a pattern, which can be used to solve the problem.

9. Guess and Check

One of the most important and effective problem-solving techniques is *Guess and Check*. It is also known as *Trial and Error*. As the name suggests, students have to guess the answer to a problem and check if that guess is correct. If the guess is wrong, students will make another guess. This will continue until the guess is correct.

It is beneficial to keep a record of all the guesses and checks in a table. In addition, a *Comments* column can be included. This will enable students to analyze their guess (if it is too high or too low) and improve on the next guess. Be careful; this problem-solving technique can be tiresome without systematic or logical guesses.

Example: Jessica had 15 coins. Some of them were 10-cent coins and the rest were 5-cent coins. The total amount added up to $1.25. How many coins of each kind were there?

Use the guess-and-check method.

Number of 10¢ Coins	Value	Number of 5¢ Coins	Value	Total Number of Coins	Total Value
7	$7 \times 10¢ = 70¢$	8	$8 \times 5¢ = 40¢$	$7 + 8 = 15$	$70¢ + 40¢ = 110¢$ = $1.10
8	$8 \times 10¢ = 80¢$	7	$7 \times 5¢ = 35¢$	$8 + 7 = 15$	$80¢ + 35¢ = 115¢$ = $1.15
10	$10 \times 10¢ = 100¢$	5	$5 \times 5¢ = 25¢$	$10 + 5 = 15$	$100¢ + 25¢ = 125¢$ = $1.25

There were **ten** 10-cent coins and **five** 5-cent coins.

10. Restate the Problem

When solving challenging math problems, conventional methods may not be workable. Instead, restating the problem will enable students to see some challenging problems in a different light so that they can better understand them.

The strategy of restating the problem is to "say" the problem in a different and clearer way. However, students have to ensure that the main idea of the problem is not altered.

How do students restate a math problem?

First, read and understand the problem. Gather the given facts and unknowns. Note any condition(s) that have to be satisfied.

Next, restate the problem. Imagine narrating this problem to a friend. Present the given facts, unknown(s), and condition(s). Students may want to write the "revised" problem. Once the "revised" problem is analyzed, students should be able to think of an appropriate strategy to solve it.

11. Simplify the Problem

One of the commonly used strategies in mathematical problem solving is simplification of the problem. When a problem is simplified, it can be "broken down" into two or more smaller parts. Students can then solve the parts systematically to get to the final answer.

Table of Contents

Singapore Math Practice Level 5A

LEARNING OUTCOMES

Unit 1   Whole Numbers (Part 1)
Students should be able to
- recognize numbers up to 10 million in words and numerals.
- recognize the place and value of each digit of the numbers.
- compare numbers up to 10 million.
- arrange numbers in order and complete number patterns.
- round numbers to the nearest thousand.
- estimate the answers for addition, subtraction, multiplication, and division problems.

Unit 2   Whole Numbers (Part 2)
Students should be able to
- perform addition, subtraction, multiplication, and division with the use of a calculator.
- perform multiplication and division of tens, hundreds, and thousands.
- estimate the values in multiplication and division problems.
- perform order of operations.
- solve story problems related to whole numbers.

Review 1
This review tests students' understanding of Units 1 & 2.

Unit 3   Fractions (Part 1)
Students should be able to
- identify like and unlike fractions.
- add and subtract unlike fractions and mixed numbers.
- make a connection between fractions and division.
- convert fractions to decimals.
- solve story problems related to fractions.

Unit 4   Fractions (Part 2)
Students should be able to
- find the product of proper fractions.
- find the product of improper and proper fractions.
- find the product of improper and improper fractions.
- find the product of mixed numbers and whole numbers.
- divide fractions by whole numbers.
- solve story problems related to fractions.

Review 2
This review tests students' understanding of Units 3 & 4.

Unit 5   Area of Triangles
Students should be able to
- identify the sides of a triangle.
- identify the base and height of a triangle.
- apply the formula to calculate the area of triangles.
- find the area of shaded triangles.

Unit 6   Ratio
Students should be able to
- find ratios and equivalent ratios.
- find the ratio of 2 or 3 given quantities.
- reduce a ratio to its simplest form.
- solve story problems related to ratios.

Review 3
This review tests students' understanding of Units 5 & 6.

Final Review
This review serves as a practice test and is an excellent assessment of students' understanding of all the topics in this book.

9

FORMULA SHEET

Unit 1 Whole Numbers (Part 1)

numerals	1	10	100	1,000	10,000	100,000	1,000,000
words	one	ten	one hundred	one thousand	ten thousand	one hundred thousand	one million
value of digit 1	1	10	100	1,000	10,000	100,000	1,000,000
place of digit 1	ones	tens	hundreds	thousands	ten thousands	hundred thousands	millions

Rules for comparing numbers
- Start from the left.
- If the values of the digits are the same, compare until they are different.

Rules for rounding numbers to the nearest thousand
- Use the approximation sign ($\approx$).
- Round up to the nearest thousand when the value of the digit in the hundreds place is 5 or more.
- Round down to the nearest thousand when the value of the digit in the hundreds place is less than 5.

When estimating the value in addition and subtraction, round the numbers before adding or subtracting.

When estimating the value in multiplication, round the multiplicand before multiplying.

When estimating the value in division, round the dividend to a number that can be divided by the divisor without any remainder.

Unit 2 Whole Numbers (Part 2)
Things to note when using a calculator

- Press $\boxed{C}$ to clear the display on the calculator before starting to key in the numbers.
- Key in the numbers and operation signs ($+$, $-$, $\times$, $\div$) on the calculator.
- Press $\boxed{=}$ to get the final answer.

Shortcuts for multiplying numbers by 10, 100, and 1,000
When multiplying numbers by 10, add a zero after the number.

When multiplying numbers by 100, add 2 zeros after the number.

When multiplying numbers by 1,000, add 3 zeros after the number.

Shortcuts for dividing numbers by 10, 100, and 1,000
When dividing numbers ending with 0 by 10, remove a zero.

When dividing numbers ending with 00 by 100, remove 2 zeros.

When dividing numbers ending with 000 by 1,000, remove 3 zeros.

Estimation in Multiplication and Division
In multiplication, round

2-digit numbers to the nearest ten,

3-digit numbers to the nearest hundred,

4-digit numbers to the nearest thousand.

In division, round

the divisor to the nearest ten,

the dividend to a number that can be divided by the divisor without any remainder.

Rules for Order of Operations
- Brackets – Solve operations in brackets first.
- Multiplication and Division – Solve operations involving multiplication and division before addition and subtraction.
- Addition and Subtraction – Solve operations involving addition and subtraction last.

* If the sum involves only addition and subtraction, or only multiplication and division, work from left to right.

Unit 3 Fractions (Part 1)
Like fractions have the same denominator.

Examples: $\frac{1}{3}$ and $\frac{2}{3}$

Unlike fractions have different denominators.

Examples: $\frac{1}{6}$ and $\frac{2}{5}$

Adding and subtracting unlike fractions
- Make sure the denominators are the same before adding or subtracting.
- In order to make the denominators common, find the common multiple of the denominators.

Fractions and Division
$$\frac{\text{Numerator}}{\text{Denominator}} = \text{Numerator} \div \text{Denominator}$$

Fractions to Decimals

Some fractions can be converted to tenths, hundredths, and thousandths before being converting to decimals.

Examples: $\frac{1}{2} = \frac{5}{10} = 0.5$

$\frac{6}{25} = \frac{24}{100} = 0.24$

$\frac{16}{125} = \frac{128}{1,000} = 0.128$

When fractions cannot be converted to tenths, hundredths, and thousandths, use long division to convert fractions to decimals.

Example:

$\frac{5}{9} = 5 \div 9 \approx 0.56$ (2 decimal places)

Convert Improper Fractions to Decimals

Convert improper fractions to whole numbers and proper fractions first.

Use long division to convert proper fractions to decimals.

Add decimals to whole numbers to get the answers.

Example:

$\frac{13}{9} = \frac{9}{9} + \frac{4}{9}$

$\approx 1 + 0.44$ (2 decimal places)

$= 1.44$

Convert Mixed Numbers to Decimals

Separate whole numbers and fractions in the mixed numbers.

Use long division to convert fractions to decimals.

Add decimals to whole numbers to get the answers.

Example:

$4\frac{1}{6} = 4 + \frac{1}{6}$

$\approx 4 + 0.17$ (2 decimal places)

$= 4.17$

Adding and subtracting mixed numbers

- First, find a common denominator for unlike fractions.
- Add or subtract the whole numbers.
- Add or subtract the fractions.
- If the final fraction becomes improper after adding, make it a proper fraction. Remember to add to the whole number.

Things to note when using a calculator for fractions

Use $\boxed{a^b/_c}$ when keying fractions.

Examples:

$\frac{1}{2}$ Press $\boxed{C}$ $\boxed{1}$ $\boxed{a^b/_c}$ $\boxed{2}$

$3\frac{1}{5}$ Press $\boxed{C}$ $\boxed{3}$ $\boxed{a^b/_c}$ $\boxed{1}$ $\boxed{a^b/_c}$ $\boxed{5}$

Unit 4 Fractions (Part 2)

Finding the product of fractions

Multiply the 2 numerators.

Multiply the 2 denominators.

Write the final answer in its simplest form.

Alternatively, when there is a common factor between the numerators and denominators, divide accordingly to make the final answer smaller.

Remember to divide only when there is a common factor between the

- numerator and denominator in a fraction.
- numerator of one fraction and denominator of another fraction.

Finding the product of mixed numbers and whole numbers

Convert the mixed number into an improper fraction.

Multiply the numerator of the fraction by the whole number.

The denominator remains the same.

Write the final answer as a mixed number.

Dividing fractions by whole numbers

Write the whole number as an improper fraction, with the whole number as the numerator and 1 as the denominator.

Change the division sign ($\div$) to a multiplication sign ($\times$).

Multiply the fractions as usual.

Unit 5 Area of Triangles

In a triangle, its height is always perpendicular to the triangle's base.

Area of triangle $= \frac{1}{2} \times$ base $\times$ height

Unit 6 Ratio

Ratio is used to show comparison between 2 or 3 quantities.

Note that ratio may not be the actual quantities being compared.

To obtain an equivalent ratio, multiply ratio by a common factor.

Similarly, we can divide ratio by a common factor to reduce it to its simplest form.

Unit 1: WHOLE NUMBERS (PART 1)

Examples:

1. Write four million, nine hundred thousand, six hundred thirteen as a numeral.

   <u>4,900,613</u>

2. Write 853,147 in words.

   <u>Eight hundred fifty-three thousand, one hundred forty-seven</u>

3. In 397,102,
   (a) what is the value of the digit 7?
   (b) in which place is the digit 9?

   (a) <u>7,000</u>
   (b) <u>ten thousands</u>

4. Which is greater 516,489 or 516,752?

   <u>516,752</u>

5. Round the numbers to the nearest thousand and estimate the value of 1,735 + 3,432.

   $1,735 + 3,432 \approx 2,000 + 3,000 =$ <u>**5,000**</u>

6. Estimate the value of 8,269 ÷ 9.

   $8,269 \div 9 \approx 8,100 \div 9 =$ <u>**900**</u>

Singapore Math Practice Level 5A

Write the following numbers as words.

1.   4,003,000 _____

2.   7,800,000 _____

3.   869,539 _____

4.   4,502,146 _____

5.   397,653 _____

Write the numbers on the lines.

6.   Two million, seven hundred six thousand   _____

7.   Four hundred eighty-three thousand   _____

8.   Eight million, three hundred fourteen   _____

9.   One hundred forty-five thousand, one   _____

10. Six million, one hundred one thousand, six hundred   _____

Fill in each blank with the correct answer.

11. In 54,617,

     (a)   the digit 7 is in the _____ place.

     (b)   the value of the digit 1 is _____.

12. In 24,367,

     (a)   the digit 4 is in the _____ place.

     (b)   the value of the digit 2 is _____.

14

13. In 512,463,

    (a) the digit _____ is in the ten thousands place.

    (b) the value of the digit 5 is _____.

14. In 208,943,

    (a) the digit _____ is in the hundred thousands place.

    (b) the digit 8 stands for _____.

15. Circle the smallest number.

    597,630   579,603   569,730

16. Circle the smallest number.

    345,028   354,280   345,208

17. Circle the largest number.

    612,011   621,101   621,110

18. Circle the largest number.

    740,877   704,788   740,787

19. $72,662 = 70,000 +$ _____ $+ 600 + 62$

20. $551,700 = 550,000 + 1,000 +$ _____

21. $1,854,000 = 1,000,000 +$ _____ $+ 4,000$

22. $4,600,800 =$ _____ $+ 600,000 + 800$

23. $1,000,000 = 999,000 +$ _____

Singapore Math Practice Level 5A

Arrange the following numbers in increasing order.

24. 35,425, 34,552, 32,554, 35,524

_____

25. 68,190, 68,091, 68,910, 68,109

_____

Arrange the following numbers in decreasing order.

26. 270,153, 207,153, 270,351, 207,531

_____

27. 419,527, 914,257, 419,257, 914,527

_____

28. 3,926,000, 3,269,000, 3,962,000, 3,296,000

_____

Complete the number patterns.

29. 66,001, 68,002, 70,003, _____, _____

30. 233,055, 234,055, _____, _____, 237,055

31. 47,405, _____, 49,405, 50,405, _____, 52,405

32. 187,310, 197,310, _____, _____, 227,310

33. 5,004,000, 5,014,000, _____, 5,034,000, _____

Singapore Math Practice Level 5A

Round the following numbers to the nearest thousand.

34. 1,563 ≈ _____

35. 5,099 ≈ _____

36. 21,459 ≈ _____

37. 708,600 ≈ _____

38. 139,999 ≈ _____

Round each number to the nearest thousand. Then, estimate the value of the following.

39. 2,157 + 6,193 ≈ _____

40. 38,500 + 18,692 ≈ _____

41. 4,165 − 2,842 ≈ _____

42. 78,213 − 18,218 ≈ _____

43. 4,915 × 5 ≈ _____

44. 8,199 × 4 ≈ _____

45. 16,003 ÷ 8 ≈ _____

46. 83,562 ÷ 7 ≈ _____

Singapore Math Practice Level 5A

Unit 2: WHOLE NUMBERS (PART 2)

Examples:

1. Solve 2,968 x 44 with the use of a calculator.

    Press $\boxed{C}$ $\boxed{2}$ $\boxed{9}$ $\boxed{6}$ $\boxed{8}$ $\boxed{\times}$ $\boxed{4}$ $\boxed{4}$ $\boxed{=}$

   130,592

2. Find the value of 368 x 1,000.

   368 x 1,000 = **368,000**

3. Find the value of 397,400 ÷ 100.

   397,400 ÷ 100 = **3,974**

4. Estimate the value of 819 x 65.

   819 x 65 ≈ 800 x 70 = **56,000**

5. Estimate the value of 5,938 ÷ 55.

   5,938 ÷ 55 ≈ 6,000 ÷ 60 = **100**

6. Solve the following problem. Use a calculator to check your answer.

    468 + (968 − 128) ÷ 6
   = 468 + 840 ÷ 6
   = 468 + 140
   = **608**

   Press $\boxed{C}$ $\boxed{4}$ $\boxed{6}$ $\boxed{8}$ $\boxed{+}$ $\boxed{(}$ $\boxed{9}$ $\boxed{6}$ $\boxed{8}$ $\boxed{-}$ $\boxed{1}$ $\boxed{2}$ $\boxed{8}$ $\boxed{)}$ $\boxed{÷}$ $\boxed{6}$ $\boxed{=}$

Singapore Math Practice Level 5A

Solve the following problems with the use of a calculator.

1. 16,259 + 508 = _____

2. 39,084 − 4,975 = _____

3. 1,020 ÷ 15 = _____

4. 96 × 73 = _____

5. 57,038 + 1,042 = _____

6. 49 × 199 = _____

7. 73,920 ÷ 88 = _____

8. 8,011 − 3,597 = _____

9. Find the sum of 1,395 g and 886 g. _____

10. Find the difference between 40,037 mi. and 13,589 mi. _____

11. Find the product of $4,334 and 17. _____

12. Find the quotient of 29,678 gal. and 22. _____

13. Find the difference between 93,788 cm and 8,134 cm. _____

14. Find the quotient of 67,598 lb. and 73. _____

15. Find the sum of $1,900,023 and $29,073. _____

Singapore Math Practice Level 5A

Write the correct answers on the lines. You may use a calculator whenever you see **.**

16. $83 \times 10 =$ _____

17. $6,004 \times 10 =$ _____

18. $196 \times 10 =$ _____

19. $39 \times 30 = 39 \times$ _____ tens $=$ _____ tens $=$ _____

20. $404 \times 90 = 404 \times$ _____ tens $=$ _____ tens $=$ _____

21. $8,644 \times 50 = 8,644 \times$ _____ tens $=$ _____ tens $=$ _____

22. $19 \times 100 =$ _____

23. $575 \times 100 =$ _____

24. $1,840 \times 100 =$ _____

25. $64 \times 1,000 =$ _____

26. $183 \times 1,000 =$ _____

27. $5,190 \times 1,000 =$ _____

28. $21 \times 400 = 21 \times$ _____ hundreds $=$ _____ hundreds $=$ _____

29. $307 \times 9,000 = 307 \times$ _____ thousands $=$ _____ thousands $=$ _____

30. $8,316 \times 700 = 8,316 \times$ _____ hundreds $=$ _____ hundreds $=$ _____

31. $50 \div 10 =$ _____

32. $410 \div 10 =$ _____

Singapore Math Practice Level 5A

33. $7{,}070 \div 10 = $ _____

34. $950 \div 50 = $ _____

35. $5{,}760 \div 90 = $ _____

36. $42{,}420 \div 70 = $ _____

37. $8{,}400 \div 100 = $ _____

38. $15{,}900 \div 100 = $ _____

39. $600 \div 100 = $ _____

40. $14{,}000 \div 700 = $ _____

41. $48{,}000 \div 600 = $ _____

42. $90{,}900 \div 300 = $ _____

43. $60{,}000 \div 1{,}000 = $ _____

44. $4{,}000 \div 1{,}000 = $ _____

45. $13{,}000 \div 1{,}000 = $ _____

46. $550{,}000 \div 5{,}000 = $ _____

47. $72{,}000 \div 8{,}000 = $ _____

48. $54{,}000 \div 6{,}000 = $ _____

49. (a) Estimate the value of $1{,}870 \times 28$. _____

    (b) Find the value of $1{,}870 \times 28$ with the use of a calculator. _____

Singapore Math Practice Level 5A

50. (a)   Estimate the value of 9,008 × 8.   _____

   (b)   Find the value of 9,008 × 8 with the use of a calculator.   _____

51. (a)   Estimate the value of 9,024 ÷ 48.   _____

   (b)   Find the value of 9,024 ÷ 48 with the use of a calculator.   _____

52. (a)   Estimate the value of 17,577 ÷ 63.   _____

   (b)   Find the value of 17,577 ÷ 63 with the use of a calculator.   _____

Solve the following problems. Use a calculator to check your answers.

53.   (35 + 15 + 20) ÷ 7 = _____

54.   (18 ÷ 3) + 32 − 10 = _____

55.   36 − (84 ÷ 12) + (14 × 5) = _____

56.   78 ÷ (456 − 450) × 90 = _____

57.   8 × (17 − 9) − 28 = _____

58.   56 ÷ 8 + 13 × (88 − 28) = _____

59.   600 + (72 − 32) ÷ 5 × 80 = _____

60.   100 ÷ 20 x (5 + 9) = _____

61.   55 ÷ (13 − 8) − 7 + 21 × 2 = _____

62.   (18 − 5) × 7 + (23 − 11) ÷ 3 = _____

Solve the following story problems. Show your work in the space below. You may use a calculator whenever you see 🖩.

63. The price of a blouse was twice the price of a skirt. Annie spent $150 on 4 blouses and 2 skirts. What was the cost of each blouse?

64. Juan bought 30 books for $7 each at a book fair. If he saved $5 per book, how much would he have paid to buy all the books at the original price?

Singapore Math Practice Level 5A

65. A baker sold 278 rolls on Tuesday. He sold 39 more rolls on Tuesday than on Monday. The number of rolls he sold on Wednesday was twice the number of rolls sold on Tuesday. How many rolls did the baker sell altogether during the 3 days?

66. Kelly had 3 times as much money as Andy. After giving Andy $450, Kelly had twice as much money as he did.

(a) How much money did Andy have in the end?

(b) How much money did Kelly have in the beginning?

Singapore Math Practice Level 5A

67. Mrs. Jackson bought 3 kg of shrimp at $22 per kg, 5 kg of crabs at $18 per kg, and some salmon at $9 per kg. If Mrs. Jackson paid $264 for the seafood, how many kilograms of salmon did she buy?

68. When 2 dozen cans of food are placed in a bucket, the mass is 4,560 g. When 18 cans of food are placed in the same bucket, the mass is 3,480 g. Find the mass of the bucket.

Singapore Math Practice Level 5A

69. Zoe bought a leather sofa and was allowed to pay for it in installments. After paying a deposit of $399, she could pay the rest in 24 monthly installments. If Zoe paid $275 every month, how much was the leather sofa?

70. Mei packed 783 strawberries equally into 9 cartons. After giving 4 cartons to her neighbors, she decided to repack 5 strawberries into each carton. How many cartons of strawberries did she have in the end?

71. Mr. Johnson imported some cartons of noodles. There were 28 packages of noodles in each carton. He then sold 10 packages of noodles for $5. If he received $280 from the sale of noodles, how many cartons of noodles did he sell?

72. A store manager bought 7 boxes of books. Each box held 25 books. He then bought 9 boxes of pencils. There were 100 pencils in each box. If the manager paid $19 for each book and $ for each pencil, how much did he pay in all?

73. There are 4 times as many yellow marbles as green marbles in a box. If there are 48 more yellow marbles than green marbles, how many marbles are there altogether in the box?

74. Grace places some plums in bags of 8 and some kiwis in bags of 4. After selling each bag of plums for $2 and each bag of kiwis for $5, she earns $2,516. If Grace sells 7 times as many bags of kiwis as bags of plums, how many pieces of fruit does she sell in all?

75. Nadia bought 5 bracelets for $2,079 each. She paid for the bracelets in 15 installments. How much did she pay for each installment?

76. A baker bought 680,000 oz. of flour and packed the flour into 200 bags of equal size. He used some flour and had 100 bags left. He decided to repack the remaining flour into bags of 5,000 oz. How many bags of flour did he have in the end?

REVIEW 1

Choose the correct answer, and write its number in the parentheses. You may use a calculator whenever you see 🖩.

1. Which of the following shows five million, twenty thousand, thirteen correctly?

    (1) 5,002,013   (3) 5,020,130

    (2) 5,020,013   (4) 5,200,013   (   )

2. Which of the following is **not** equal to 70 × 190?

    (1) 700 × 19   (3) 10 × 70 × 90

    (2) 190 × 7 × 10   (4) 7 × 19 × 100   (   )

3. Which of the following is the best estimate for 15,469 ÷ 45?

    (1) 15,000 ÷ 40   (3) 16,000 ÷ 40

    (2) 15,000 ÷ 50   (4) 16,000 ÷ 50   (   )

4. What is the value of 36 + 6 ÷ 3 × 4 − 11?

    (1) 33   (3) 45

    (2) 44   (4) 108   (   )

5. In 748,120, which digit is in the hundred thousands place?

    (1) 8   (3) 4

    (2) 7   (4) 1   (   )

6. What does the digit 8 stand for in 6,908,135?

    (1) 800,000   (3) 8,000

    (2) 80,000   (4) 800   (   )

Singapore Math Practice Level 5A

7. The owner of a toy store had 2,234 blue marbles and 7,586 yellow marbles. He sold 1,680 marbles and packed the remaining marbles equally into 44 packages. How many marbles were there in each package?

    (1) 180   (3) 261

    (2) 185   (4) 262   (   )

Write your answers on the lines. You may use a calculator whenever you see .

8. Write 6,100,049 in words.

    _____

9. In 2,076,953, which digit is in the ten thousands place?   _____

10. Round 14,397 to the nearest thousand.   _____

11. Estimate the value of 52,452 ÷ 84.   _____

12. What is the value of 31 × (6 + 8) ÷ 2 − 60 ÷ 15?   _____

13. Find the product of 308 and 67.   _____

14. Complete the number pattern.

    80,125, 81,359, _____, 83,827, 85,061   _____

15. What is the value of 76,400 ÷ 400?   _____

Singapore Math Practice Level 5A

Solve the following story problems. Show your work in the space below. You may use a calculator whenever you see ▧.

▧ 16. Mr. Delgado installed the cabinets in his kitchen. He paid a deposit of $520 and paid the rest in monthly installments of $315 for 2 years. How much did it cost to install the cabinets?

17. A factory produced 15,300 T-shirts in January. It produced 2,500 more T-shirts in February than in January. It produced twice the number of T-shirts in March as it did in February. What was the total number of T-shirts the factory produced during these 3 months?

Singapore Math Practice Level 5A

18. On a farm, there are a total of 50 cows and chickens. These animals have 124 legs in all. How many more chickens than cows are there?

19. There were a total of 625 goldfish and guppies in an aquarium. There were 79 more guppies than goldfish. Mr. Goldberg put an equal number of goldfish into 21 bags and sold 10 bags of goldfish. How many more guppies than goldfish were left?

Singapore Math Practice Level 5A

20. Alina bought 32 boxes of greeting cards. She rearranged the greeting cards into packs of 3 and sold each pack for $10. She received $960 from the sale. How many greeting cards were there in each box?

Unit 3: FRACTIONS (PART 1)

Examples:

1. $\frac{1}{9} + \frac{2}{3} = \frac{1}{9} + \frac{6}{9} = \frac{7}{9}$

2. $\frac{3}{4} - \frac{1}{8} = \frac{6}{8} - \frac{1}{8} = \frac{5}{8}$

3. Write $18 \div 7$ as a fraction in its simplest form. Change the fraction to a mixed number.

   $18 \div 7 = \frac{18}{7} = 2\frac{4}{7}$

4. Convert $\frac{5}{11}$ to a decimal. Round your answer to 2 decimal places.

   $5 \div 11 \approx 0.454 = \underline{\textbf{0.45}}$

5. $5\frac{1}{2} + 13\frac{1}{6} = 5\frac{3}{6} + 13\frac{1}{6} = 18\frac{4}{6} = \underline{\textbf{18}\frac{2}{3}}$

6. $4\frac{3}{4} - 2\frac{1}{2} = 4\frac{3}{4} - 2\frac{2}{4} = 2\frac{1}{4}$

Singapore Math Practice Level 5A

Identify the like fractions in each set.

1. $\frac{1}{8}, \frac{1}{4}, \frac{1}{2}, \frac{2}{5}, \frac{4}{8}$

_____

2. $\frac{3}{6}, \frac{1}{3}, \frac{5}{6}, \frac{4}{12}, \frac{4}{6}$

_____

3. $\frac{1}{4}, \frac{3}{4}, \frac{1}{12}, \frac{3}{8}, \frac{6}{10}$

_____

Identify the unlike fractions in each set.

4. $\frac{4}{10}, \frac{1}{5}, \frac{5}{10}, \frac{8}{10}, \frac{3}{7}$

_____

5. $\frac{3}{7}, \frac{1}{3}, \frac{6}{7}, \frac{1}{5}, \frac{7}{9}$

_____

6. $\frac{5}{9}, \frac{1}{11}, \frac{8}{11}, \frac{3}{8}, \frac{1}{2}$

_____

Add the unlike fractions. Write your answer in its simplest form.

7. $\frac{1}{5} + \frac{4}{6} =$

8. $\frac{2}{7} + \frac{2}{3} =$

9. $\frac{1}{8} + \frac{1}{2} =$

10. $\frac{6}{12} + \frac{1}{6} =$

11. $\frac{3}{4} + \frac{2}{10} =$

Singapore Math Practice Level 5A

Subtract the unlike fractions. Write your answer in its simplest form.

12. $\dfrac{2}{3} - \dfrac{4}{7} =$

13. $\dfrac{2}{9} - \dfrac{1}{12} =$

14. $\dfrac{3}{5} - \dfrac{1}{4} =$

15. $\dfrac{8}{9} - \dfrac{2}{5} =$

16. $\dfrac{5}{6} - \dfrac{4}{7} =$

Solve the following problems. Write your answer as a fraction in its simplest form or as a mixed number.

17. $12 \div 8 =$

18. $29 \div 5 =$

19. $\dfrac{36}{7} =$

20. $\dfrac{42}{4} =$

Convert the following fractions to decimals. Round your answer to 2 decimal places. You may use a calculator whenever you see 🖩.

21. $\dfrac{5}{20} =$

22. $\dfrac{4}{7} \approx$

Singapore Math Practice Level 5A

23. $6\frac{2}{9} \approx$

24. $\frac{3}{8} \approx$

25. $\frac{9}{11} \approx$

26. $13\frac{1}{3} \approx$

Add the mixed numbers. Write your answer in its simplest form. You may use a calculator whenever you see ▨.

27. $2\frac{7}{8} + 1\frac{1}{3} =$

28. $4\frac{4}{9} + 1\frac{3}{4} =$

29. $10\frac{2}{5} + 3\frac{2}{7} =$

30. $3\frac{1}{6} + 5\frac{5}{9} =$

31. $3\frac{2}{3} + 4\frac{4}{5} =$

32. $9\frac{6}{7} + 2\frac{1}{4} =$

Subtract the mixed numbers. Write your answer in its simplest form. You may use a calculator whenever you see ▨.

33. $5\frac{3}{5} - 1\frac{3}{10} =$

34. $4\frac{9}{10} - 2\frac{2}{3} =$

Singapore Math Practice Level 5A

35. $6\frac{3}{11} - 3\frac{1}{2} =$

36. $2\frac{4}{5} - 1\frac{3}{4} =$

37. $4\frac{1}{7} - 3\frac{1}{3} =$

38. $12\frac{5}{8} - 4\frac{3}{4} =$

Solve the following story problems. Show your work in the space below. You may use a calculator whenever you see ▦.

39. Peter bikes from his house to the library. After biking for $3\frac{2}{5}$ mi., he still has to bike for another $2\frac{1}{2}$ mi. in order to reach the library. How far is his house from the library?

Singapore Math Practice Level 5A

40. Nadeem spent $\frac{3}{5}$ of his money on books. He spent another $\frac{2}{7}$ of his money on art supplies. What fraction of his money did he have left?

41. Taliyah bought a piece of rope that was $3\frac{4}{9}$ yd. long. Luke bought a piece of rope that was $\frac{3}{5}$ yd. shorter than Taliyah's. What was the total length of rope Taliyah and Luke bought?

Singapore Math Practice Level 5A

42. Clara took $1\frac{1}{4}$ hours to finish her Math homework. She took $\frac{5}{6}$ hours longer to finish her English homework. How long did Clara take to finish all her homework?

43. The total mass of a watermelon, a papaya, and a honeydew melon is $6\frac{1}{2}$ kg. The watermelon has a mass of $3\frac{3}{4}$ kg. The papaya has a mass that is $1\frac{7}{8}$ kg lighter than the watermelon. What is the mass of the honeydew melon?

Singapore Math Practice Level 5A

44. Nicholas bought 5 pizzas. After his sisters had eaten some, there were $3\frac{3}{4}$ pizzas left. Nicholas ate $\frac{7}{8}$ fewer pizzas than his sisters. How many pizzas did they eat altogether?

45. Emilia prepared 9 quarts of syrup. She poured them equally into 4 containers and gave 1 container of syrup to her neighbor. How many quarts of syrup did her neighbor receive?

Unit 4: FRACTIONS (PART 2)

Examples:

1. Find the value of $\frac{4}{9}$ of $\frac{2}{7}$.

    $$\frac{4}{9} \text{ of } \frac{2}{7} = \frac{4}{9} \times \frac{2}{7}$$
    $$= \frac{4 \times 2}{9 \times 7}$$
    $$= \underline{\frac{8}{63}}$$

2. $\dfrac{2}{9} \times \dfrac{10}{8} = \dfrac{\overset{1}{2} \times 10}{9 \times \underset{4}{8}}$

    $$= \frac{10}{36}$$
    $$= \underline{\frac{5}{18}}$$

3. $5\frac{1}{4} \times 10 = \frac{21}{4} \times 10$

    $$= \frac{21 \times 10}{4}$$
    $$= \frac{210}{4}$$
    $$= 52\frac{2}{4}$$
    $$= \underline{52\frac{1}{2}}$$

4. $\dfrac{4}{5} \div 3 = \dfrac{4}{5} \times \dfrac{1}{3}$

    $$= \frac{4 \times 1}{5 \times 3}$$
    $$= \underline{\frac{4}{15}}$$

Singapore Math Practice Level 5A

Multiply these proper fractions. Write your answer in its simplest form.

1. $\dfrac{4}{9} \times \dfrac{3}{8} =$ _____

2. $\dfrac{5}{12} \times \dfrac{4}{7} =$ _____

3. $\dfrac{2}{5} \times \dfrac{6}{10} =$ _____

4. $\dfrac{11}{12} \times \dfrac{3}{9} =$ _____

5. $\dfrac{8}{9} \times \dfrac{3}{4} =$ _____

6. $\dfrac{2}{5} \times \dfrac{2}{3} =$ _____

Multiply the improper fractions by the proper fractions. You may use a calculator whenever you see **.**

7. $\dfrac{4}{7} \times \dfrac{9}{5} =$ _____

8. $\dfrac{10}{11} \times \dfrac{21}{6} =$ _____

9. $\dfrac{3}{8} \times \dfrac{15}{2} =$ _____

10. $\dfrac{18}{4} \times \dfrac{2}{9} =$ _____

11. $\dfrac{7}{3} \times \dfrac{1}{8} =$ _____

12. $\dfrac{23}{5} \times \dfrac{10}{12} =$ _____

Singapore Math Practice Level 5A

Multiply the improper fractions by the improper fractions. You may use a calculator whenever you see 🖩.

13. $\frac{13}{10} \times \frac{20}{8} =$ _____

14. $\frac{10}{3} \times \frac{21}{5} =$ _____

🖩 15. $\frac{49}{9} \times \frac{30}{7} =$ _____

16. $\frac{9}{2} \times \frac{13}{6} =$ _____

🖩 17. $\frac{15}{11} \times \frac{35}{12} =$ _____

🖩 18. $\frac{33}{8} \times \frac{41}{7} =$ _____

Multiply the mixed numbers by the whole numbers. You may use a calculator whenever you see 🖩.

19. $2\frac{3}{5} \times 40 =$ _____

20. $6\frac{1}{8} \times 18 =$ _____

🖩 21. $8\frac{2}{7} \times 56 =$ _____

🖩 22. $99 \times 5\frac{7}{11} =$ _____

23. $16 \times 3\frac{1}{3} =$ _____

🖩 24. $74 \times 4\frac{5}{6} =$ _____

Singapore Math Practice Level 5A

Divide these fractions. Write your answer in its simplest form.

25. $\dfrac{3}{4} \div 6 = $ _____

26. $\dfrac{5}{8} \div 10 = $ _____

27. $\dfrac{4}{11} \div 2 = $ _____

28. $\dfrac{6}{9} \div 4 = $ _____

29. $\dfrac{2}{9} \div 12 = $ _____

30. $\dfrac{6}{7} \div 6 = $ _____

Solve the following story problems. Show your work in the space below. You may use a calculator whenever you see 🖩.

31. A bag of hazelnuts has a mass of 15 oz. The mass of a bag of cashews is $\dfrac{2}{5}$ that of the bag of hazelnuts.

    (a) What is the total mass of the hazelnuts and cashews?
    (b) The nuts are mixed together and packed equally into 8 packages. What is the mass of each package of mixed nuts?

Singapore Math Practice Level 5A

32. Mr. Mulvaney earns $4,815 every month. He saves $\frac{2}{9}$ of it and spends $\frac{1}{2}$ of the remaining money on food. How much does he spend on food?

33. After Jamal spent $\frac{3}{8}$ of his money and Caroline spent $\frac{3}{8}$ of her money, Jamal had $40 more than Caroline. How much more money did Jamal have than Caroline in the beginning?

Singapore Math Practice Level 5A

34. Bella lost $\frac{1}{3}$ of her marbles in a game. She gave $\frac{2}{5}$ of the remaining marbles to her sister and put the rest of the marbles equally into 4 pouches. If each pouch contained 72 marbles, how many marbles did she have in the beginning?

35. Isaiah and Andy had a total of 560 trading cards. After Isaiah gave $\frac{1}{9}$ of his trading cards to Andy, they had an equal number of trading cards. How many more trading cards did Isaiah have than Andy in the beginning?

Singapore Math Practice Level 5A

36. The width of Field A is $\frac{7}{12}$ of its length of 108 m. What is the perimeter of Field B if it has $\frac{5}{6}$ of the perimeter of Field A?

37. There are 1,400 students in a school. The number of girls is $\frac{3}{4}$ the number of boys. How many students are in the other grade levels if $\frac{1}{6}$ of the girls and $\frac{1}{5}$ of the boys are in first grade?

Singapore Math Practice Level 5A

38. Anna-Maria gave $\frac{3}{7}$ of her orange juice to her brother. She drank $\frac{1}{4}$ of the remaining orange juice. What fraction of the orange juice did she have left?

39. Elle had $840. She spent $\frac{5}{12}$ of the money on some clothes. $\frac{7}{10}$ of the money she spent on clothes was used to purchase 4 dresses of the same price. How much did each dress cost?

Singapore Math Practice Level 5A

40. Lara had some money in her savings account. She withdrew $\frac{3}{8}$ of it and spent $\frac{2}{9}$ of the withdrawal on some books. She gave $\frac{4}{7}$ of the remaining money to her mother and banked the rest of the money. If Lara banked $756, how much money did she have in her savings account in the beginning?

41. Akiko bought 32 packages of red beans. The mass of each package of red beans was $45\frac{3}{4}$ oz.
    (a) What was the total mass of all 32 packages of red beans?
    (b) If Akiko gave $\frac{1}{3}$ of the red beans to her neighbor, how much did she have left?

Singapore Math Practice Level 5A

42. $\frac{3}{7}$ of the muffins in a bakery were carrot muffins. The number of blueberry muffins was twice the number of multi-grain muffins. The number of multi-grain muffins was $\frac{1}{3}$ the number of banana muffins. If there were 108 multi-grain muffins, how many carrot muffins were there?

REVIEW 2

Choose the correct answer, and write its number in the parentheses. You may use a calculator whenever you see 🖩.

1. Which of the following is an unlike fraction?

   (1) $\dfrac{1}{7}$ (3) $\dfrac{4}{7}$

   (2) $\dfrac{3}{8}$ (4) $\dfrac{6}{7}$ (   )

🖩 2. Convert $21\dfrac{1}{9}$ into decimal.

   (1) 21.10   (3) 21.19

   (2) 21.11   (4) 21.99   (   )

3. Multiply $\dfrac{6}{11}$ by $\dfrac{2}{5}$.

   (1) $\dfrac{8}{55}$ (3) $\dfrac{52}{55}$

   (2) $\dfrac{12}{55}$ (4) $\dfrac{15}{11}$ (   )

4. $2\dfrac{4}{5} + 4\dfrac{2}{3} = $ _____

   (1) $6\dfrac{7}{15}$ (3) $7\dfrac{1}{15}$

   (2) $6\dfrac{8}{15}$ (4) $7\dfrac{7}{15}$ (   )

5. Ashley poured $\dfrac{9}{10}$ L of milk equally into 3 glasses. How much milk was there in each glass?

   (1) $\dfrac{3}{10}$ L   (3) $2\dfrac{7}{10}$ L

   (2) $\dfrac{3}{5}$ L   (4) $3\dfrac{9}{10}$ L   (   )

Singapore Math Practice Level 5A

6. Find the value of $\frac{4}{9} \div 12$.

    (1) $\frac{1}{27}$ (3) $5\frac{1}{3}$

    (2) $\frac{3}{16}$ (4) $12\frac{4}{9}$ (   )

7. For which of the following multiplication sentences is the product $\frac{3}{2}$?

    (1) $\frac{1}{4} \times \frac{12}{8}$ (3) $\frac{9}{12} \times \frac{3}{5}$

    (2) $\frac{8}{11} \times \frac{33}{4}$ (4) $\frac{4}{11} \times \frac{33}{8}$ (   )

Write your answers on the lines. You may use a calculator whenever you see .

8. Identify the like fractions.

    $\frac{3}{10} , \frac{1}{10} , \frac{1}{3} , \frac{6}{9}$ _____

 9. Find the value of $14\frac{5}{9} \times 81$.   _____

10. Mrs. Lee had 9 sandwiches. She distributed the sandwiches equally among her 4 children. How many sandwiches did each child get? Write your answer in its simplest form.

                                                                                             _____

11. Multiply $\frac{12}{5}$ by $\frac{3}{2}$. Write your answer as a mixed number.   _____

12. Find the value of $\frac{1}{2} - \frac{3}{7}$.   _____

13. Find the product of $\frac{2}{7}$ and $\frac{3}{10}$.   _____

Singapore Math Practice Level 5A

14. What is $\frac{1}{11}$ of $654? Write your answer as a decimal and round it to 2 decimal places.

_____

15. Find the value of $8\frac{7}{12} - 5\frac{1}{3}$.

_____

Solve the following story problems. Show your work in the space below. You may use a calculator whenever you see ▧.

16. Bailey gave 10 packets of stickers to Anna. Each packet contained 15 stickers. $\frac{2}{5}$ were animal stickers and $\frac{5}{6}$ of the remaining stickers were flower stickers. The rest of the stickers were scented. How many scented stickers were there?

Singapore Math Practice Level 5A

17. A container holds $5\frac{1}{5}$ L of water. A bottle holds $3\frac{1}{2}$ L less water than the container. Water from the container and the bottle are mixed and poured equally into 30 glasses. How much water does each glass contain? Write your answer in milliliters.

18. The owner of a fruit stand had some mangoes. $\frac{2}{9}$ of the mangoes were rotten. He gave 18 mangoes to his neighbor and sold 7 times as many mangoes as he gave away. If he had $\frac{1}{3}$ of the mangoes left, how many mangoes did he have in the beginning?

19. Eduardo had some marbles. $\frac{2}{5}$ of them were blue, $\frac{5}{9}$ of the remaining marbles were green, and the rest were purple. There were 32 fewer purple marbles than blue marbles. How many marbles did Eduardo have in the beginning?

20. Mrs. Pappas had some apples. She sold $\frac{1}{3}$ of the apples plus 5 more on the first day. She sold $\frac{1}{3}$ of the remaining apples plus 5 more on the second day. She had 125 apples left in the end. How many apples did Mrs. Pappas have in the beginning?

Singapore Math Practice Level 5A

Unit 5: AREA OF TRIANGLES

1.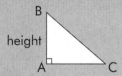

Identify the base for the given height in the triangle.

Base = __AC__

2.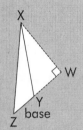

Identify the height for the given base in the triangle.

Height = __XW__

3. Find the area of the triangle MNO.

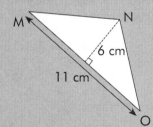

$$\text{Area of triangle MNO} = \frac{1}{2} \times \text{base} \times \text{height}$$
$$= \frac{1}{2} \times 11 \times 6$$
$$= \underline{\mathbf{33 \ cm^2}}$$

4. Find the area of the shaded triangle.

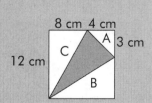

$$\text{Area of A} = \frac{1}{2} \times 4 \times 3 = 6 \ cm^2$$

$$\text{Area of B} = \frac{1}{2} \times (12 - 3) \times (8 + 4) = 54 \ cm^2$$

$$\text{Area of C} = \frac{1}{2} \times 8 \times 12 = 48 \ cm^2$$

$$\text{Area of square} = 12 \times 12 = 144 \ cm^2$$

$$\text{Area of shaded area} = 144 - (6 + 54 + 48)$$
$$= \underline{\mathbf{36 \ cm^2}}$$

Singapore Math Practice Level 5A

Name the 3 sides of each triangle. Identify its base and height.

1.

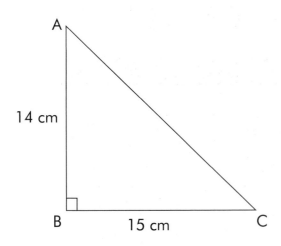

The 3 sides of the triangle are

_____, _____, and _____.

Base = _____ = _____ cm

Height = _____ = _____ cm

2.

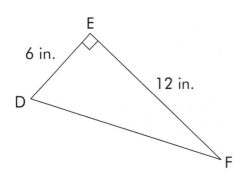

The 3 sides of the triangle are

_____, _____, and _____.

Base = _____ = _____ in.

Height = _____ = _____ in.

3.

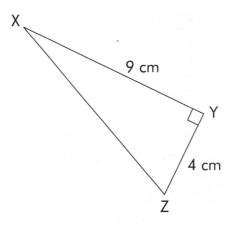

The 3 sides of the triangle are

_____, _____, and _____.

Base = _____ = _____ cm

Height = _____ = _____ cm

Singapore Math Practice Level 5A

Find the area of each triangle.

4.

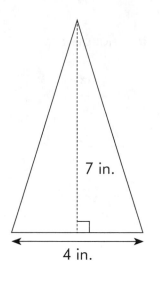

7 in.

4 in.

Base = _____ in.

Height = _____ in.

Area = _____ in.²

5.

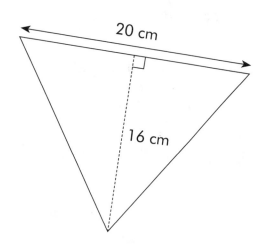

20 cm

16 cm

Base = _____ cm

Height = _____ cm

Area = _____ cm²

6.

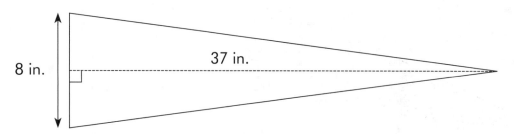

8 in.

37 in.

Base = _____ in.

Height = _____ in.

Area = _____ in.²

For each figure, find the area of the shaded triangle.

7.

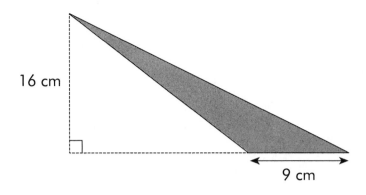

_____

8.

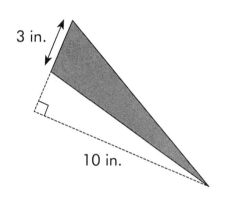

_____

9.

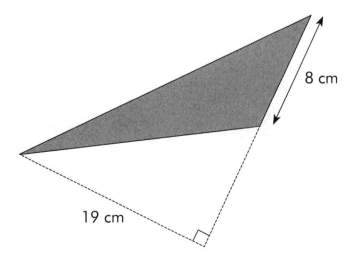

_____

Singapore Math Practice Level 5A

10.

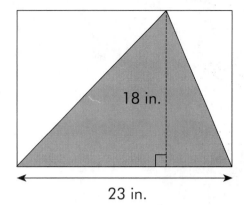

18 in.

23 in.

_____

11.

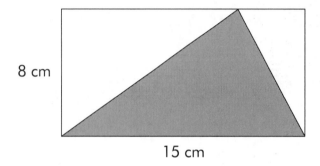

8 cm

15 cm

_____

12.

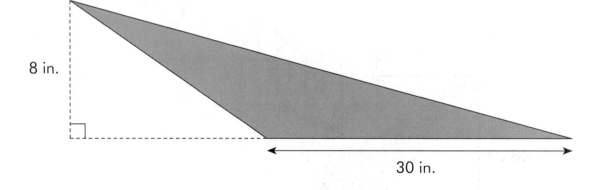

8 in.

30 in.

_____

13.

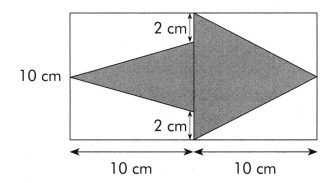

14.

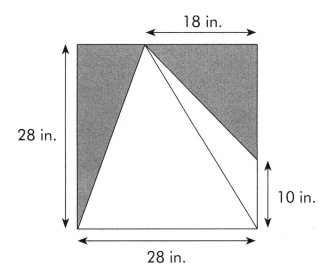

15.

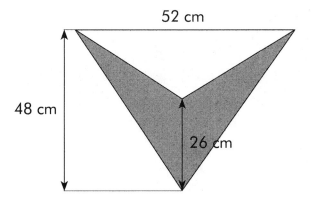

Write your answers on the lines.

16. The figure below is made of 8 identical rectangles, each measuring 4 in. by 6 in. Find the area of the shaded triangles.

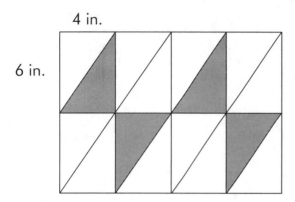

_____

17. The figure below is made of 4 identical triangles. Find the area of the shaded triangles.

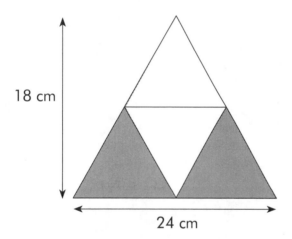

_____

18. The figure below is made of 3 triangles. Find its area.

16 in.   20 in.

3 in.   7 in.

16 in.   20 in.

_____

19. The figure below is made of 4 identical triangles. Find its area.

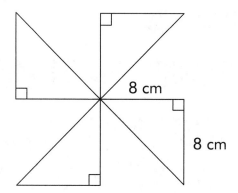

8 cm

8 cm

20. The figure below is made of 5 identical triangles. Find its area.

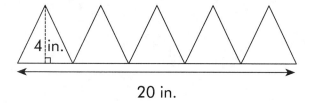

4 in.

20 in.

Singapore Math Practice Level 5A

Unit 6: RATIO

1. The table below shows the different sports played by a class of students.

Sports	Baseball	Swimming	Karate	Track & Field
Number of students	8	15	9	7

   (a) Find the ratio of students who do karate to the students who swim.

   (b) Find the ratio of students who like track and field to the students who play baseball.

   (a) number of students who do karate : number of students who swim

   $$9 : 15$$
   $$\underline{3 : 5}$$

   (b) number of students who like track and field : number of students who play baseball

   $$\underline{7 : 8}$$

2. Complete the equivalent ratio.

   $$5 : 8$$
   $$25 : \underline{40}$$

3. George has 8 bags of marbles and 5 bags of ping pong balls. There are 6 marbles in each bag and 12 ping pong balls in each bag.

   (a) Find the ratio of marbles to ping pong balls.

   (b) Find the ratio of bags of ping pong balls to bags of marbles.

   (a) $$8 \times 6 = 48$$

   There are 48 marbles altogether.

   $$5 \times 12 = 60$$

   There are 60 ping pong balls altogether.

   number of marbles : number of ping pong balls

   $$48 : 60$$
   $$\underline{4 : 5}$$

   (b) number of bags of ping pong balls : number of bags of marbles

   $$\underline{5 : 8}$$

Singapore Math Practice Level 5A

Fill in each blank with a ratio in its simplest form.

1.

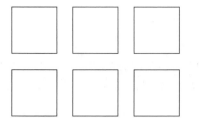 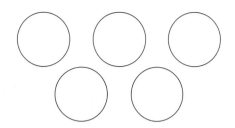

The ratio of squares to circles is _____.

The ratio of circles to squares is _____.

2.

The ratio of pencils to erasers is _____.

The ratio of erasers to pencils is _____.

3.

The ratio of chickens to ducks is _____.

The ratio of ducks to chickens is _____.

Singapore Math Practice Level 5A

4.
Stick A
_____
30 in.

Stick B
_____
45 in.

The ratio of the length of Stick A to the length of Stick B is _____.

The ratio of the length of Stick B to the length of Stick A is _____.

5.

The ratio of the mass of the watermelon to the mass of the papaya is _____.

The ratio of the mass of the papaya to the mass of the watermelon is _____.

6.

8 in.

A   5 in.

4 in.

B   8 in.

(a)   The ratio of the perimeter of Rectangle A to the perimeter of Rectangle B is _____.

The ratio of the perimeter of Rectangle B to the perimeter of Rectangle A is _____.

(b)   The ratio of the area of Rectangle A to the area of Rectangle B is _____.

The ratio of the area of Rectangle B to the area of Rectangle A is _____.

Singapore Math Practice Level 5A

Write each ratio in its simplest form. You may use a calculator whenever you see .

7.   21 : 27 = _____

8.   18 : 63 = _____

9.   64 : 56 = _____

10. 25 : 120 = _____

11. 84 : 60 = _____

12. 90 : 50 : 60 = _____

13. 36 : 54 : 108 = _____

14. 45 : 95 : 70 = _____

15. 91 : 78 : 65 = _____

16. 100 : 75 : 225 = _____

Fill in the missing number in each equivalent ratio. You may use a calculator whenever you see .

17. 8 : 5 = 40 : _____

18. 6 : 7 = 18 : _____

19. 9 : _____ = 108 : 96

Singapore Math Practice Level 5A

20. $54 : \underline{\hspace{2cm}} = 9 : 6$

21. $\underline{\hspace{2cm}} : 8 = 77 : 88$

 22. $\underline{\hspace{2cm}} : 24 : \underline{\hspace{2cm}} = 8 : 6 : 3$

23. $3 : 7 : 4 = 27 : \underline{\hspace{2cm}} : \underline{\hspace{2cm}}$

24. $2 : 9 : 5 = \underline{\hspace{2cm}} : 45 : \underline{\hspace{2cm}}$

 25. $\underline{\hspace{2cm}} : \underline{\hspace{2cm}} : 3 = 60 : 96 : 36$

26. $\underline{\hspace{2cm}} : 6 : \underline{\hspace{2cm}} = 72 : 48 : 56$

Write your answers on the lines. You may use a calculator whenever you see .

27. There are 26 boys on a school bus carrying 42 students.

    (a) What is the ratio of boys to the total number of students on the school bus?

    _____

    (b) What is the ratio of girls to boys on the school bus?

    _____

28. There are 46 books and half as many comic books on a shelf. What is the ratio of comic books to the total number of books on the shelf?

    _____

Singapore Math Practice Level 5A

29. Town A is 15 mi. away from the hospital. Town B is 24 mi. away from the hospital. What is the ratio of the distance from Town A to the hospital to the distance from Town A to Town B?

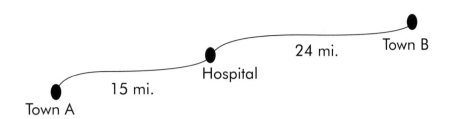

_____

30. The table below shows the postage for mail to England.

Types of mail	Postage
Postcards	$0.80
Letters	$1.45
Packages up to 200 g	$5
Packages up to 500 g	$9

(a) What is the ratio of the postage for a postcard to the postage for a letter?

_____

(b) What is the ratio of the postage for a 200-g package to the postage for a 300-g package?

_____

(c) What is the ratio of the postage for 3 postcards to the postage for a 450-g package?

_____

71

31.

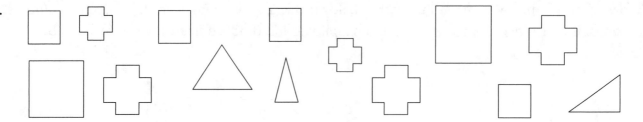

What is the ratio of triangles to squares to crosses?

_____

32.

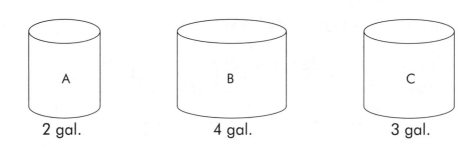

What is the ratio of the capacity of Container A to the capacity of Container C to the total capacity of the 3 containers?

_____

33. The admission price to a concert is shown below.

Adult	$57
Child	$24
Senior citizen	$42

What is the ratio of the price of a ticket for a senior citizen to the price of a ticket for an adult to the price of a ticket for a child?

_____

Singapore Math Practice Level 5A

34.

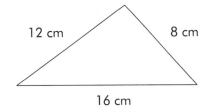

12 cm   8 cm

16 cm

What is the ratio of the length of the longest side to the length of the shortest side of the triangle shown above?

_____

Solve the following story problems. Show your work in the space below. You may use a calculator whenever you see .

35. The ratio of adults to children in a library is 5 : 6. If there are 102 children in the library, how many people are there in the library altogether?

Singapore Math Practice Level 5A

36. The ratio of boots to sandals in a shoe store is 8 : 3. If there are 245 more boots than sandals in the store, how many boots are there?

37. During the summer, Addison babysits for kids in her neighborhood. The ratio of her earnings for a weekday to her earnings for a weekend is 3 : 4. If she is paid $42 on a weekday, how much does she earn for working on Saturday and Sunday?

38. There are 22 roses, 12 daisies, and 16 carnations in a bouquet.

    (a) What is the ratio of roses to the total number of flowers in the bouquet?

    (b) How many carnations must be added to the bouquet so that the ratio of daisies to carnations becomes 1 : 3?

39. Jasmine bought 3,500 g of flour. She used $\frac{3}{7}$ of it to bake some tarts and 700 g of flour to bake a cake. Find the ratio of flour used for baking the cake to flour used for baking the tarts to the remaining flour.

Singapore Math Practice Level 5A

40. Peter, Anya, and Oliver share a sum of money in the ratio 2 : 5 : 4.

   (a) If Peter receives $72, how much is the sum of money?
   (b) How much must Anya give to Peter so that they both will get an equal share?

41. The ratio of stamps that Trina has to stamps that Madison has is 7 : 6. The ratio of stamps that Madison has to those that Li has is 3 : 5. What is the ratio of stamps that Li has to the total number of stamps the 3 girls have?

Singapore Math Practice Level 5A

42. The ratio of the price of an adult train ticket to the price of a child's train ticket is 8 : 5. Mr. Tanaka pays $64 for 2 adult train tickets. How much is the cost of a child's train ticket?

REVIEW 3

Choose the correct answer, and write its number in the parentheses. You may use a calculator whenever you see 📟**.**

1. $5 : 7 = $ _____ $: 21$

    (1)   3   (3)   12

    (2)   10   (4)   15   (   )

2. Alex has 46 bills and coins. If he has 18 coins, what is the ratio of bills to coins?

    (1)   9 : 14   (3)   14 : 9

    (2)   9 : 23   (4)   14 : 23   (   )

3. Molly and Alyssa shared a sum of money in the ratio 4 : 9. If Alyssa received $72, how much did Molly receive?

    (1) $32   (3) $104

    (2) $36   (4) $108   (   )

4. What is the area of the shaded triangle?

    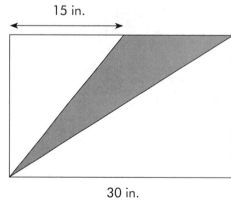

    (1)   120 in.²   (3)   300 in.²

    (2)   150 in.²   (4)   600 in.²   (   )

Singapore Math Practice Level 5A

5. Rose and Kylie have a total of 96 stamps. If Rose has 48 more stamps than Kylie, what is the ratio of Kylie's stamps to Rose's stamps?

(1) 1 : 2   (3) 1 : 4

(2) 1 : 3   (4) 3 : 1   (   )

6. Penny is 3 years and 6 months old. She is 1 year older than Henry. What is the ratio of Penny's age to Henry's age?

(1) 5 : 7   (3) 7 : 9

(2) 7 : 5   (4) 9 : 7   (   )

7. What is the area of the triangle shown below?

(1) 72 cm²

(2) 144 cm²

(3) 288 cm²

(4) 576 cm²

12 cm

24 cm   (   )

Write your answers on the lines. You may use a calculator whenever you see 📟.

8. Write 15 : 42 : 36 in its simplest form.   _____

9. The ratio of teachers to students in a school is 3 : 20. If there are 690 teachers and students in the school, how many students are there?

_____

10. There are 18 boys and 24 girls in a reading club. What is the ratio of girls to the total number of children in the reading club?

_____

11. Meena cuts a 287-in. long ribbon into 2 pieces in the ratio 3 : 4. What is the length of the longer piece of ribbon?

_____

79

12. Find the ratio of squares to triangles to circles shown below.

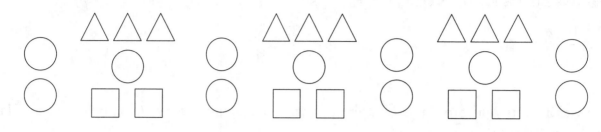

_____

13. 5 out of every 8 books in a library are fiction. The rest of the books are nonfiction. If there are 12,560 fiction books, how many nonfiction books are there?

_____

14. Find the area of the shaded triangle.

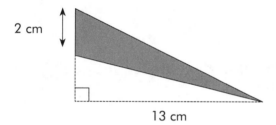

2 cm

13 cm

_____

15. Find the area of the shaded triangle.

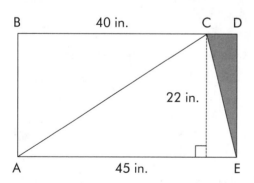

B   40 in.   C   D

22 in.

A   45 in.   E

_____

Singapore Math Practice Level 5A

Solve the following story problems. Show your work in the space below. You may use a calculator whenever you see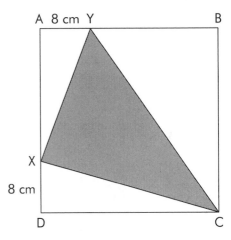

16. The perimeter of square ABCD is 96 cm. AY and XD are both 8 cm. Find the area of the shaded triangle.

17. The ratio of Japanese tourists to British tourists to German tourists in a hotel was 5 : 3 : 2. If there were 970 tourists altogether in the hotel, how many fewer German tourists than Japanese tourists were there?

81

Singapore Math Practice Level 5A

18. The ratio of the perimeters of 2 squares is 5 : 7. The perimeter of the larger square is 252 in. What is the length of a side of the smaller square?

19. The figure below is made of 4 identical triangles. Find the area of each triangle.

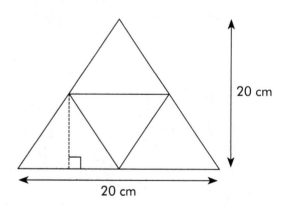

Singapore Math Practice Level 5A

20. The ratio of footballs to basketballs in a sporting goods store is 3 : 5. A total of 406 balls are purchased from the supplier. There are now 4 times as many footballs and twice as many basketballs in the store. What is the total number of footballs and basketballs in the store now?

FINAL REVIEW

Choose the correct answer, and write its number in the parentheses. Do not use a calculator.

1. Which digit in 9,403,512 is in the ten thousands place?

   (1) 0

   (2) 3

   (3) 4

   (4) 9

   (   )

2. In the figure below, which line is the base of triangle BCD?

   (1) BD

   (2) AC

   (3) BC

   (4) CD

   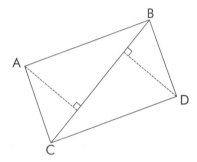

   (   )

3. A triangle has a base of 4 in. Its height is half as long as its base. The area of the triangle is
   _____.

   (1) 4 in.²

   (2) 8 in.²

   (3) 16 in.²

   (4) 32 in.²

   (   )

4. Estimate the value of 9,859 ÷ 9.

   (1) 1,000

   (2) 1,088

   (3) 1,095

   (4) 1,100

   (   )

5. Tamika has a mass of 36 kg and Tricia has a mass of 54 kg. What is the ratio of Tamika's mass to the total mass of both girls?

   (1) 2 : 3

   (2) 2 : 5

   (3) 3 : 5

   (4) 5 : 2

   (   )

6. 51,125, 53,625, _____, 58,625, 61,125

   Complete the number pattern.

   (1) 54,125   (3) 56,125

   (2) 54,625   (4) 56,625   (   )

7. $125 \times 69 = $ _____

   (1) 8,500   (3) 8,750

   (2) 8,625   (4) 8,875   (   )

8. At a bookfair, Carmen sold 4,938 novels on Friday and 6,054 novels on Saturday. She found that she still had 19,835 novels left. How many novels did she have in the beginning?

   (1) 10,992   (3) 25,889

   (2) 24,773   (4) 30,827   (   )

9. $8\frac{4}{5}$ of 30 has the value of _____.

   (1) 246   (3) 264

   (2) 260   (4) 266   (   )

10. Which of the following shows nine million, ninety thousand, nine hundred nine correctly?

    (1) 9,009,090   (3) 9,090,909

    (2) 9,090,099   (4) 9,900,909   (   )

11. ABCD is a square that measures 12 in. on each side. Lines AC and BD divide the square into 4 identical triangles. Find the area of triangle DAB.

    (1) 18 in.²

    (2) 36 in.²

    (3) 72 in.²

    (4) 144 in.²   (   )

12. Write 250 cents as a ratio of $10.

    (1) 1 : 4   (3) 2 : 5

    (2) 1 : 25   (4) 4 : 1   (   )

Singapore Math Practice Level 5A

13. Write $7\frac{5}{7}$ as a decimal. Round the answer to 2 decimal places.

    (1) 7.57   (3) 7.71

    (2) 7.70   (4) 7.75   ( )

14. $12\frac{1}{5} - 5\frac{1}{10} = $ _____

    (1) $6\frac{9}{10}$ (3) $7\frac{1}{10}$

    (2) 7   (4) $17\frac{3}{10}$ ( )

15. At a camera store, $6,384 was collected from the sale of film which was sold in boxes of 2 rolls each. How many rolls of film were sold altogether if the price of each box of film was $21?

    (1) 152   (3) 456

    (2) 304   (4) 608   ( )

Write your answers on the lines.

16. The population of a city is 195,643. Round the population of the city to the nearest thousand.

                                                                  _____

17. What does the digit 7 stand for in 1,073,564?   

18. Find the area of the shaded triangle.

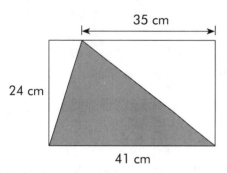

                                                                  _____

19. There are 42 students in the class. If 8 students fail a test, what is the ratio of students who fail the test to students who pass the test?

                                                                  _____

Singapore Math Practice Level 5A

20. Find the area of the triangle.

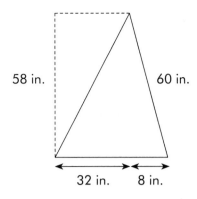

58 in.   60 in.

32 in.   8 in.

_____

21. Max baked 84 boxes of muffins. There were 12 muffins in each box. He sold each muffin for $2. How much money would he make if he sold all the muffins?

_____

22. Find the area of the shaded triangle.

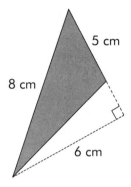

5 cm

8 cm

6 cm

_____

23. Find the value of $4\frac{6}{8} \times 12$.   _____

24. Write three million, five hundred nine thousand as a numeral.

_____

25. Jasmine mixes 3,750 mL of lemonade concentrate with 8,750 mL of water. The mixture can fill 10 identical bottles completely. What is the capacity of each bottle? Write your answer in liters.

_____

Singapore Math Practice Level 5A

26. $18 : 30 : 72 = 6 : \boxed{} : 24$

What is the missing number in the box?

_____

27. Vijay ate $\dfrac{3}{11}$ of a pizza and gave a quarter of the remaining pizza to his sister. What fraction of the pizza did he have left?

_____

28. Mrs. Campbell bought 3 kg of sugar. She used $\dfrac{3}{4}$ of it. How many grams of sugar did she have left?

_____

29. Derrick is 8 years old. He is 32 years younger than his father. Write the ratio of Derrick's age to his father's age.

_____

30. Find the value of $80 \times (69 + 22) - 288$. _____

Write your answers on the lines. You may use a calculator.

31. Solve $75 \times 3 + 108 \div (27 \div 3)$. _____

32. Multiply 949 by 86. _____

33. Solve $\dfrac{36}{5} + \dfrac{29}{9}$. _____

34. Divide 3,528 by 36. _____

35. 7 girls shared $\dfrac{3}{4}$ of a loaf of banana bread equally. What fraction of the banana bread did each girl receive?

_____

36. 3 plates and 4 cups cost $35.50, while 3 plates and 3 cups cost $31.50. What is the cost of 9 plates?

37. The figure below shows an octagon made of 8 identical triangles. Find the area of the octagon if each triangle has a base of 5 cm and a height of 8 cm.

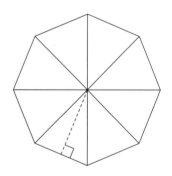

38. A tour package to Japan costs $2\frac{1}{2}$ times as much as a tour package to Indonesia. The tour package to Japan costs $\frac{5}{7}$ times as much as a tour package to England. If the cost of the Indonesian tour package is $880, find the total cost of all 3 tour packages.

39. The total mass of 3 baskets of vegetables is $21\frac{3}{5}$ lb. Basket A has a mass of $6\frac{1}{4}$ lb. and Basket B has a mass of $2\frac{7}{8}$ lb. more than Basket A. What is the difference between the mass of the heaviest and the lightest baskets of vegetables?

40. The ratio of the sides of 2 squares is 7 : 9. The perimeter of the smaller square is 112 cm. What is the difference in the area of the 2 squares?

41. Chloe bought an equal number of forks and spoons for a party. The forks were sold at 3 for $2 and the spoons were sold at 4 for $3. She spent $5 more on spoons than on forks. How much did she spend altogether?

Singapore Math Practice Level 5A

42. Last year, $\frac{1}{4}$ of the members in a health club were women. When 56 women joined the club, the fraction of women in the health club became $\frac{5}{6}$. How many men were there in the health club?

43. Jason used $\frac{3}{7}$ of a pile of paper for a project. Olivia used $\frac{1}{6}$ of the remaining pile of paper for the same project. If there were 90 pieces of unused paper, how many pieces of paper were there in the beginning?

Singapore Math Practice Level 5A

44. The ratio of Michael's points on an English test to Paloma's points on the same test is 12 : 11. The ratio of Michael's points on the English test to Anton's points on the same test is 4 : 3. The 3 students score a total of 224 points on the same test. What is the difference between Paloma's and Anton's points on the English test?

45. A salesperson had to sell 50 watches for his company every month. For every watch he sold, he earned $34. In addition, he had to buy every unsold watch from his company for $68. If he made $986 at the end of a month, how many watches were not sold that month?

Singapore Math Practice Level 5A

46. Tierra had 5 times as many trading cards as Patrick. Tierra gave $\frac{1}{4}$ of her trading cards to Patrick. Patrick then gave $\frac{1}{3}$ of his trading cards to Tierra. If Tierra had 96 more trading cards than Patrick in the end, how many trading cards did she have in the beginning?

47. Julia's age is $\frac{1}{5}$ of her grandmother's age. 5 years ago, her grandmother was 60 years old.

   (a)   Write Julia's age 5 years ago as a ratio of her grandmother's age 5 years ago.

   (b)   In how many years will Julia's age be $\frac{2}{5}$ of her grandmother's present age?

Singapore Math Practice Level 5A

48. The ratio of Aaron's money to David's money was 7 : 4. When Aaron spent $6 and David's mother gave David another $36, they had the same amount of money. How much did each of them have in the beginning?

CALCULATOR SKILLS

Solve the following problems using a calculator.

1. $852 \times 11 = $ _____

2. $9{,}719 \times 63 = $ _____

3. $420 \div 12 = $ _____

4. $6{,}762 \div 23 = $ _____

5. $71 + 13 - 9 = $ _____

6. $562 + 112 \div 7 = $ _____

7. $25 \times (35 + 18) = $ _____

8. $3{,}600 \div (982 - 622) = $ _____

9. $(149 - 126 + 78) \times 420 \div 5 = $ _____

10. $6{,}978 - 15 \times (22 \times 19 \div 3) = $ _____

Rewrite the following fractions as decimals using a calculator. Round each answer to 2 decimal places.

11. $\frac{4}{9} \approx$ _____

12. $\frac{6}{11} \approx$ _____

13. $\frac{1}{8} \approx$ _____

14. $7\frac{1}{9} \approx$ _____

15. $13\frac{8}{11} \approx$ _____

Solve the following problems using a calculator.

16. $5\frac{1}{2} + 9\frac{1}{4} =$ _____

17. $22\frac{1}{6} + 14\frac{1}{8} =$ _____

18. $49\frac{3}{7} + 60\frac{5}{11} =$ _____

19. $78\frac{5}{6} - 34\frac{7}{10} =$ _____

20. $53\frac{1}{4} - 8\frac{2}{9} =$ _____

21. $\frac{14}{8} \times \frac{5}{6} =$ _____

22. $\frac{26}{5} \times \frac{3}{2} =$ _____

Singapore Math Practice Level 5A

23. $\dfrac{88}{12} \times \dfrac{16}{3} =$ _____

24. $\dfrac{21}{5} \times \dfrac{2}{3} =$ _____

25. $1\dfrac{3}{8} \times 64 =$ _____

26. $5\dfrac{1}{10} \times 95 =$ _____

27. $104 \times 16\dfrac{2}{3} =$ _____

28. $21 \times 6\dfrac{8}{9} =$ _____

29. $\dfrac{1}{4} \div 8 =$ _____

30. $\dfrac{5}{12} \div 10 =$ _____

31. $\dfrac{9}{10} \div 3 =$ _____

32. $\dfrac{6}{11} \div 2 =$ _____

33. $\dfrac{7}{9} \div 14 =$ _____

34. $\dfrac{3}{4} \div 24 =$ _____

35. $\dfrac{2}{5} \div 6 =$ _____

Singapore Math Practice Level 5A

CHALLENGE QUESTIONS

Solve the following problems on another sheet of paper.

1. Look at the pattern below. Fill in each empty box with the correct answer.

1,234	973,626	789
2,345		678
3,456		567

2. I am a 7-digit number. All my digits are different. The first, third, fifth, and last digits are all even numbers. The rest of the digits are odd numbers. When you add each digit to the next digit, you will get 975,979. What am I?

3. Grandma wants to distribute an orange equally among 4 grandchildren. Her grandchildren challenge her to cut the orange with the least number of cuts. Explain how Grandma can meet the challenge.

4. The ratio of stamps collected by Kofi to the stamps collected by Marcus is 1 : 2. The ratio of stamps collected by Marcus to stamps collected by Andy is 5 : 7. If the difference between the number of stamps collected by Marcus and Andy is 144, what is the difference between the number of stamps collected by Kofi and Andy?

5. Fill in the empty box with the correct answer.

6	2	8
10	18	28
46		120

6. The total number of coins in Containers A, B, and C is 1,020. The number of coins in Container A is 136 fewer than the number of coins in Container B. The number of coins in Container C is 136 more than the number of coins in Container B. What is the ratio of coins in Container A to coins in Container B to coins in Container C?

Singapore Math Practice Level 5A

7. The figure below is made of 5 identical triangles and 1 larger triangle. Find the area of each unshaded triangle if y is $\frac{2}{3}$ the height of the larger big triangle.

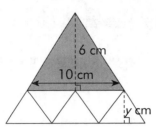

8. Keiko earns a 4-digit salary. The first digit is $\frac{2}{3}$ of the second digit. The second digit is $\frac{3}{4}$ of the third digit, and the third digit is $1\frac{3}{5}$ of the last digit. If the last digit is 5, how much does Keiko earn?

9. M is a number between 60 and 90. When M is divided by 4, it has a remainder of 3. When M is divided by 5, it has a remainder of 3. What is M?

10. The height of triangle ABC is 8 in. Its base is $1\frac{3}{4}$ as long as its height. Find the shaded area if y is $\frac{3}{4}$ the height of triangle ABC.

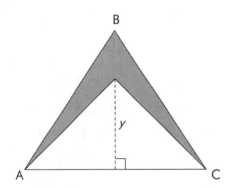

11. Kelly is 5 years older than Maya. Maya is $\frac{3}{4}$ as old as Connor. The total age of the 3 siblings is 65. Who is the oldest among the 3 of them? What is the age of the oldest person?

12. I am a 4-digit number. The ratio of my first digit to my second digit is 3 : 1. The ratio of my third digit to my last digit is 1 : 3. The ratio of my first digit to my last digit is 2 : 3. If all my digits add up to 20, what number am I?

Singapore Math Practice Level 5A

Unit 1: Whole Numbers (Part 1)

1. **Four million, three thousand**
2. **Seven million, eight hundred thousand**
3. **Eight hundred sixty-nine thousand, five hundred thirty-nine**
4. **Four million, five hundred two thousand, one hundred forty-six**
5. **Three hundred ninety-seven thousand, six hundred fifty-three**
6. **2,706,000**
7. **483,000**
8. **8,000,314**
9. **145,001**
10. **6,101,600**
11. $54,617 = 50,000 + 4,000 + 600 + 10 + 7$
    (a) **ones**
    (b) **10**
12. $24,367 = 20,000 + 4,000 + 300 + 60 + 7$
    (a) **thousands**
    (b) **20,000**
13. $512,463 = 500,000 + 10,000 + 2,000 + 400 + 60 + 3$
    (a) **1**
    (b) **500,000**
14. $208,943 = 200,000 + 8,000 + 900 + 40 + 3$
    (a) **2**
    (b) **8,000**
15. **569,730**
    597,630   579,603   5⑥9,730
    In the ten thousands place, the digit 6 is the smallest.
16. **345,028**
    345,⓪28   354,280   345,208
    Comparing 345,028 and 345,208, the digit 0 in the hundreds place is smaller.
17. **621,110**
    612,011   621,101   621,1①0
    Comparing 621,101 and 621,110, the digit 1 in the tens place is greater.
18. **740,877**
    740,⑧77   704,788   740,787
    Comparing 740,877 and 740,787, the digit 8 in the hundreds place is greater.
19. **2,000**
    $72,662 = 70,000 + 2,000 + 600 + 62$
20. **700**
    $551,700 = 550,000 + 1,000 + 700$
21. **850 000**
    $1,854,000 = 1,000,000 + 850,000 + 4,000$
22. **4 000 000**
    $4,600,800 = 4,000,000 + 600,000 + 800$
23. **1,000**
    $1,000,000 - 999,000 = 1,000$
24. **32,554, 34,552, 35,425, 35,524**
    32,554 is the smallest and 35,524 is the largest.
    34,552 is smaller than 35,425.
25. **68,091, 68,109, 68,190, 68,910**
    68,091 is the smallest and 68,910 is the largest.
    68,109 is smaller than 68,190.

26. **270,351, 270,153, 207,531, 207,153**
    270,351 is the largest and 207,153 is the smallest.
    270,153 is greater than 207,531.
27. **914,527, 914,257, 419,527, 419,257**
    914,527 is the largest and 419,257 is the smallest.
    914,257 is greater than 419,527.
28. **3,962,000, 3,926,000, 3,296,000, 3,269,000**
    3,962,000 is the largest and 3,269,000 is the smallest.
    3,926,000 is greater than 3,296,000.
29. **72,004, 74,005**
    $70,003 - 68,002 = 2,001$
    $70,003 + 2,001 = 72,004$
    $72,004 + 2,001 = 74,005$
30. **235,055 , 236,055**
    $234,055 - 233,055 = 1,000$
    $234,055 + 1,000 = 235,055$
    $235,055 + 1,000 = 236,055$
31. **48,405 , 51,405**
    $50,405 - 49,405 = 1,000$
    $47,405 + 1,000 = 48,405$
    $50,405 + 1,000 = 51,405$
32. **207,310 , 217,310**
    $197,310 - 187,310 = 10,000$
    $197,310 + 10,000 = 207,310$
    $207,310 + 10,000 = 217,310$
33. **5,024,000, 5,044,000**
    $5,014,000 - 5,004,000 = 10,000$
    $5,014,000 + 10,000 = 5,024,000$
    $5,034,000 + 10,000 = 5,044,000$
34. **2,000**
    1,563 is nearer to 2,000 than to 1,000.
35. **5,000**
    5,099 is nearer to 5,000 than to 6,000.
36. **21,000**
    21,459 is nearer to 21,000 than to 22,000.
37. **709,000**
    708,600 is nearer to 709,000 than to 708,000.
38. **140,000**
    139,999 is nearer to 140,000 than to 139,000.
39. **8,000**
    $2,157 + 6,193 \approx 2,000 + 6,000 = 8,000$
40. **58,000**
    $38,500 + 18,692 \approx 39,000 + 19,000 = 58,000$
41. **1,000**
    $4,165 - 2,842 \approx 4,000 - 3,000 = 1,000$
42. **60,000**
    $78,213 - 18,218 \approx 78,000 - 18,000 = 60,000$
43. **25,000**
    $4,915 \times 5 \approx 5,000 \times 5 = 25,000$
44. **32,000**
    $8,199 \times 4 \approx 8,000 \times 4 = 32,000$
45. **2,000**
    $16,003 \div 8 \approx 16,000 \div 8 = 2,000$
46. **12,000**
    $83,562 \div 7 \approx 84,000 \div 7 = 12,000$

1. **16,767**
   `C` `1` `6` `2` `5` `9` `+` `5` `0` `8` `=`

2. **34,109**
   `C` `3` `9` `0` `8` `4` `–` `4` `9` `7` `5` `=`

3. **68**
   `C` `1` `0` `2` `0` `÷` `1` `5` `=`

4. **7,008**
   `C` `9` `6` `×` `7` `3` `=`

5. **58,080**
   `C` `5` `7` `0` `3` `8` `+` `1` `0` `4` `2` `=`

6. **9,751**
   `C` `4` `9` `×` `1` `9` `9` `=`

7. **840**
   `C` `7` `3` `9` `2` `0` `÷` `8` `8` `=`

8. **4,414**
   `C` `8` `0` `1` `1` `–` `3` `5` `9` `7` `=`

9. **2,281 g**
   `C` `1` `3` `9` `5` `+` `8` `8` `6` `=`

10. **26,448 mi.**
    `C` `4` `0` `0` `3` `7` `–` `1` `3` `5` `8` `9` `=`

11. **$73,678**
    `C` `4` `3` `3` `4` `×` `1` `7` `=`

12. **1,349 gal.**
    `C` `2` `9` `6` `7` `8` `÷` `2` `2` `=`

13. **85,654 cm**
    `C` `9` `3` `7` `8` `8` `–` `8` `1` `3` `4` `=`

14. **926 lb.**
    `C` `6` `7` `5` `9` `8` `÷` `7` `3` `=`

15. **$1,929,096**
    `C` `1` `9` `0` `0` `0` `2` `3` `+` `2` `9` `0` `7` `3` `=`

16. **830**
    $83 \times 10 = 830$

17. **60,040**
    $6,004 \times 10 = 60,040$

18. **1,960**
    $196 \times 10 = 1,960$

19. **3, 117, 1,170**
    $39 \times 3 \text{ tens} = 117 \text{ tens} = 1,170$

20. **9, 3,636, 36,360**
    $404 \times 9 \text{ tens} = 3,636 \text{ tens} = 36,360$

21. **5, 43,220, 432,200**
    $8,644 \times 5 \text{ tens} = 43,220 \text{ tens} = 432,200$

22. **1,900**
    $19 \times 100 = 1,900$

23. **57,500**
    $575 \times 100 = 57,500$

24. **184,000**
    $1,840 \times 100 = 184,000$

25. **64,000**
    $64 \times 1,000 = 64,000$

26. **183,000**
    $183 \times 1,000 = 183,000$

27. **5,190,000**
    $5,190 \times 1,000 = 5,190,000$

28. **4, 84, 8,400**
    $21 \times 4 \text{ hundreds} = 84 \text{ hundreds} = 8,400$

29. **9, 2,763, 2,763,000**
    $307 \times 9 \text{ thousands} = 2,763 \text{ thousands}$
    $= 2,763,000$

30. **7, 58,212, 5,821,200**
    $8,316 \times 7 \text{ hundreds} = 58,212 \text{ hundreds}$
    $= 5,821,200$

31. **5**
    $50 \div 10 = 5$

32. **41**
    $410 \div 10 = 41$

33. **707**
    $7,070 \div 10 = 707$

34. **19**
    $950 \div 10 \div 5 = 95 \div 5 = 19$

35. **64**
    $5,760 \div 10 \div 9 = 576 \div 9 = 64$

36. **606**
    $42,420 \div 10 \div 7 = 4,242 \div 7 = 606$

37. **84**
    $8,400 \div 100 = 84$

38. **159**
    $15,900 \div 100 = 159$

39. **6**
    $600 \div 100 = 6$

40. **20**
    $14,000 \div 100 \div 7 = 140 \div 7 = 20$

41. **80**
    $48,000 \div 100 \div 6 = 480 \div 6 = 80$

42. **303**
    $90,900 \div 100 \div 3 = 909 \div 3 = 303$

43. **60**
    $60,000 \div 1,000 = 60$

44. **4**
    $4,000 \div 1,000 = 4$

45. **13**
    $13,000 \div 1,000 = 13$

46. **110**
    $550,000 \div 1,000 \div 5 = 550 \div 5 = 110$

47. **9**
    $72,000 \div 1,000 \div 8 = 72 \div 8 = 9$

48. **9**
    $54,000 \div 1,000 \div 6 = 54 \div 6 = 9$

49. (a) **60,000**
    $1,870 \times 28 \approx 2,000 \times 30$
    $= 2,000 \times 3 \times 10$
    $= 6,000 \times 10$
    $= 60,000$

    (b) **52,360**
    `C` `1` `8` `7` `0` `×` `2` `8` `=`

50. (a) **90,000**
    $9,008 \times 8 \approx 9,000 \times 10 = 90,000$

    (b) **72,064**
    `C` `9` `0` `0` `8` `×` `8` `=`

51. (a) **180**
    $9,024 \div 48 \approx 9,000 \div 50 = 180$

    (b) **188**
    `C` `9` `0` `2` `4` `÷` `4` `8` `=`

52. (a) **300**
    $17,577 \div 63 \approx 18,000 \div 60 = 300$

    (b) **279**
    `C` `1` `7` `5` `7` `7` `÷` `6` `3` `=`

53. **10**
    $(35 + 15 + 20) \div 7 = 70 \div 7 = 10$

For checking
C (3 5 + 1 5 + 2 0) ÷ 7 =

54. **28**
$(18 ÷ 3) + 32 - 10 = 6 + 32 - 10$
$= 38 - 10$
$= 28$

For checking
C (1 8 ÷ 3) + 3 2 - 1 0 =

55. **99**
$36 - (84 ÷ 12) + (14 × 5) = 36 - 7 + 70$
$= 29 + 70$
$= 99$

For checking
C 3 6 - (8 4 ÷ 1 2) + (1 4 × 5) =

56. **1,170**
$78 ÷ (456 - 450) × 90 = 78 ÷ 6 × 90$
$= 13 × 90$
$= 1,170$

For checking
C 7 8 ÷ (4 5 6 - 4 5 0) × 9 0 =

57. **36**
$8 × (17 - 9) - 28 = 8 × 8 - 28$
$= 64 - 28$
$= 36$

For checking
C 8 × (1 7 - 9) - 2 8 =

58. **787**
$56 ÷ 8 + 13 × (88 - 28) = 56 ÷ 8 + 13 × 60$
$= 7 + 13 × 60$
$= 7 + 780$
$= 787$

For checking
C 5 6 ÷ 8 + 1 3 × (8 8 - 2 8) =

59. **1,240**
$600 + (72 - 32) ÷ 5 × 80 = 600 + 40 ÷ 5 × 80$
$= 600 + 8 × 80$
$= 600 + 640$
$= 1,240$

For checking
C 6 0 0 + (7 2 - 3 2) ÷ 5 × 8 0 =

60. **70**
$100 ÷ 20 × (5 + 9) = 100 ÷ 20 × 14$
$= 5 × 14$
$= 70$

For checking
C 1 0 0 ÷ 2 0 × (5 + 9) =

61. **46**
$55 ÷ (13 - 8) - 7 + 21 × 2 = 55 ÷ 5 - 7 + 21 × 2$
$= 11 - 7 + 42$
$= 4 + 42$
$= 46$

For checking
C 5 5 ÷ (1 3 - 8) - 7 + 2 1 × 2 =

62. **95**
$(18 - 5) × 7 + (23 - 11) ÷ 3 = 13 × 7 + 12 ÷ 3$
$= 91 + 4$
$= 95$

For checking
C (1 8 - 5) × 7 + (2 3 - 1 1) ÷ 3 =

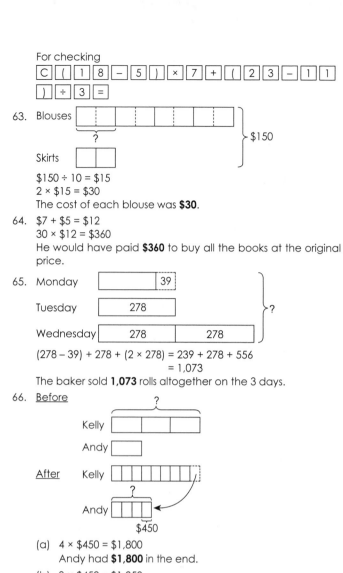

63. Blouses
?
$150
Skirts
$150 ÷ 10 = 15
$2 × $15 = 30
The cost of each blouse was **$30**.

64. $7 + $5 = 12
$30 × $12 = 360
He would have paid **$360** to buy all the books at the original price.

65. Monday 39
Tuesday 278
Wednesday 278 278
?
$(278 - 39) + 278 + (2 × 278) = 239 + 278 + 556$
$= 1,073$
The baker sold **1,073** rolls altogether on the 3 days.

66. Before
?
Kelly
Andy
After Kelly
?
Andy
$450
(a) $4 × $450 = $1,800$
Andy had **$1,800** in the end.
(b) $3 × $450 = $1,350$
$3 × $1,350 = $4,050$
Kelly had **$4,050** in the beginning.

67. $$264 - (3 × $22) - (5 × $18) = 108
$$108 ÷ $9 = 12$
She bought **12 kg** of salmon.

68. $24 - 18 = 6$ cans of food
$4,560 - 3,480 = 1,080$ g
The mass of 6 cans of food is 1,080 g.
$3,480 - (3 × 1,080) = 240$ g
The mass of the bucket is **240 g**.

69. $(24 × $275) + $399 = $6,999$
The leather sofa was **$6,999**.

70. $783 ÷ 9 = 87$
$9 - 4 = 5$
$5 × 87 = 435$
She had 435 strawberries left.
$435 ÷ 5 = 87$
She had **87** cartons of strawberries in the end.

71. $$280 ÷ $5 = 56$
$56 × 10 = 560$
$560 ÷ 28 = 20$
He sold **20** cartons of noodles.

72. $7 × 25 = 175$
$9 × 100 = 900$
$(175 × $19) + (900 × $2) = $5,125$
He paid **$5,125** in all.

73. Yellow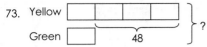

Green

$48 ÷ 3 = 16$
$5 × 16 = 80$
There are **80** marbles altogether in the box.

74. (7 × 4) kiwis + 8 plums = 28 kiwis + 8 plums
(7 × $5) + $2 = $37
$2,516 ÷ $37 = 68
68 × (28 kiwis + 8 plums)
= 1,904 kiwis + 544 plums = 2,448
She sold **2,448** pieces of fruit in all.

75. 5 × $2,079 = $10,395
$10,395 ÷ 15 = $693
She paid **$693** for each installment.

76. 680,000 ÷ 200 = 3,400
The mass of each bag of flour is 3,400 oz.
100 × 3,400 = 340,000
340,000 ÷ 5,000 = 68
He had **68** bags of flour in the end.

Review 1

1. **(2)**
5,020,013

2. **(3)**
70 × 190 = 13,300
700 × 19 = 13,300
190 × 7 × 10 = 13,300
10 × 70 × 90 = 63,000
7 × 19 × 100 = 13,300

3. **(2)**
Round 15,469 to 15,000.
Round 45 to 50.

4. **(1)**
Press C 3 6 + 6 ÷ 3 × 4 – 1 1 =

5. **(2)**

Hundred Thousands	Ten Thousands	Thousands	Hundreds	Tens	Ones
7	4	8	1	2	0

6. **(3)**
In 6,908,135, the digit 8 stands for 8,000.

7. **(2)**
2,234 + 7,586 = 9,820
9,820 – 1,680 = 8,140
8,140 ÷ 44 = 185

8. **Six million, one hundred thousand, forty-nine**

9. **7**

Millions	Hundred Thousands	Ten Thousands	Thousands	Hundreds	Tens	Ones
2	0	7	6	9	5	3

10. **14,000**
14,397 ≈ 14,000

11. **650**
52,452 ÷ 84 ≈ 52,000 ÷ 80 = 650

12. **213**
Press C 3 1 × (6 + 8) ÷ 2 – 6 0
÷ 1 5 =

13. **20,636**
Press C 3 0 8 × 6 7 =

14. **82,593**
81,359 – 80,125 = 1,234
85,061 – 83,827 = 1,234
1,234 + 81,359 = 82,593

15. **191**
76,400 ÷ 400 = 76,400 ÷ 4 ÷ 100
= 19,100 ÷ 100
= 191

16. 2 × 12 × $315 = $7,560
$7,560 + $520 = $8,080
It cost **$8,080** to install the cabinets.

17. January

February

March

$(4 × 15,300) + (3 × 2,500) = 68,700$
The total number of T-shirts the factory produced during these 3 months was **68,700**.

18. Use the Guess and Check method.

Guess	No. of cows	No. of chickens	Total number of legs	Comments
1	25	25	(25 × 4) + (25 × 2) = 150	Too high
2	20	30	(20 × 4) + (30 × 2) = 140	Too high
3	15	35	(15 × 4) + (35 × 2) = 130	Very Near
4	12	38	(12 × 4) + (38 × 2) = 124	Correct

38 – 12 = 26
There are **26** more chickens than cows.

19. 625 – 79 = 546
546 ÷ 2 = 273
There were 273 goldfish in the beginning.
273 + 79 = 352
There were 352 guppies in the beginning.
273 ÷ 21 = 13
21 – 10 = 11
11 × 13 = 143
There were 143 goldfish left in the end.
352 – 143 = 209
209 more guppies than goldfish were left.

20. $960 ÷ $10 = 96
96 × 3 = 288
288 ÷ 32 = 9
There were **9** greeting cards in each box.

Unit 3: Fractions (Part 1)

1. $\frac{1}{8}, \frac{4}{8}$

2. $\frac{3}{6}, \frac{5}{6}, \frac{4}{6}$

3. $\frac{1}{4}, \frac{3}{4}$

4. $\frac{1}{5}, \frac{3}{7}$

5. $\frac{1}{3}, \frac{1}{5}, \frac{7}{9}$

6. $\frac{5}{9}, \frac{3}{8}, \frac{1}{2}$

7. $\frac{13}{15}$

$\frac{1}{5} + \frac{4}{6} = \frac{6}{30} + \frac{20}{30} = \frac{26}{30} = \frac{13}{15}$

Singapore Math Practice Level 5A

8. $\dfrac{20}{21}$

$\dfrac{2}{7} + \dfrac{2}{3} = \dfrac{6}{21} + \dfrac{14}{21} = \dfrac{20}{21}$

9. $\dfrac{5}{8}$

$\dfrac{1}{8} + \dfrac{1}{2} = \dfrac{1}{8} + \dfrac{4}{8} = \dfrac{5}{8}$

10. $\dfrac{2}{3}$

$\dfrac{6}{12} + \dfrac{1}{6} = \dfrac{6}{12} + \dfrac{2}{12} = \dfrac{8}{12} = \dfrac{2}{3}$

11. $\dfrac{19}{20}$

$\dfrac{3}{4} + \dfrac{2}{10} = \dfrac{15}{20} + \dfrac{4}{20} = \dfrac{19}{20}$

12. $\dfrac{2}{21}$

$\dfrac{2}{3} - \dfrac{4}{7} = \dfrac{14}{21} - \dfrac{12}{21} = \dfrac{2}{21}$

13. $\dfrac{5}{36}$

$\dfrac{2}{9} - \dfrac{1}{12} = \dfrac{8}{36} - \dfrac{3}{36} = \dfrac{5}{36}$

14. $\dfrac{7}{20}$

$\dfrac{3}{5} - \dfrac{1}{4} = \dfrac{12}{20} - \dfrac{5}{20} = \dfrac{7}{20}$

15. $\dfrac{22}{45}$

$\dfrac{8}{9} - \dfrac{2}{5} = \dfrac{40}{45} - \dfrac{18}{45} = \dfrac{22}{45}$

16. $\dfrac{11}{42}$

$\dfrac{5}{6} - \dfrac{4}{7} = \dfrac{35}{42} - \dfrac{24}{42} = \dfrac{11}{42}$

17. $1\dfrac{1}{2}$

$12 \div 8 = \dfrac{12}{8} = \dfrac{3}{2} = 1\dfrac{1}{2}$

18. $5\dfrac{4}{5}$

$29 \div 5 = \dfrac{29}{5} = 5\dfrac{4}{5}$

19. $5\dfrac{1}{7}$

$\dfrac{36}{7} = 5\dfrac{1}{7}$

20. $10\dfrac{1}{2}$

$\dfrac{42}{4} = 10\dfrac{2}{4} = 10\dfrac{1}{2}$

21. **0.25**

$\dfrac{5}{20} = \dfrac{25}{100} = 0.25$

22. **0.57**

$\dfrac{4}{7} = 4 \div 7$
$= 0.571$
≈ 0.57

```
      0.5 7 1
   7 ) 4.0
     - 3 5
        5 0
      - 4 9
          1 0
        -  7
           3
```

23. **6.22**

$\dfrac{2}{9} = 2 \div 9 \approx 0.222$

$6\dfrac{2}{9} \approx 6 + 0.22 = 6.22$

```
        0.2 2 2
     9 ) 2.0
       - 1 8
          2 0
        - 1 8
           2 0
         - 1 8
            2
```

24. **0.38**

$\dfrac{3}{8} = 3 \div 8$

Press C 3 ÷ 8 =

$\dfrac{3}{8} = 0.375 \approx 0.38$

25. **0.82**

$\dfrac{9}{11} = 9 \div 11$

Press C 9 ÷ 1 1 =

$\dfrac{9}{11} = 0.8181... \approx 0.82$

26. **13.33**

$\dfrac{1}{3} = 1 \div 3$

Press C 1 ÷ 3 =

$\dfrac{1}{3} = 0.3333... \approx 0.33$

$13\dfrac{1}{3} \approx 13 + 0.33 \approx 13.33$

27. $4\dfrac{5}{24}$

$2\dfrac{7}{8} + 1\dfrac{1}{3} = 2\dfrac{21}{24} + 1\dfrac{8}{24}$
$= 3\dfrac{29}{24}$
$= 4\dfrac{5}{24}$

28. $6\dfrac{7}{36}$

$4\dfrac{4}{9} + 1\dfrac{3}{4} = 4\dfrac{16}{36} + 1\dfrac{27}{36}$
$= 5\dfrac{43}{36}$
$= 6\dfrac{7}{36}$

29. $13\dfrac{24}{35}$

$10\dfrac{2}{5} + 3\dfrac{2}{7} = 10\dfrac{14}{35} + 3\dfrac{10}{35}$
$= 13\dfrac{24}{35}$

30. $8\dfrac{13}{18}$

$3\dfrac{1}{6} + 5\dfrac{5}{9} = 3\dfrac{6}{36} + 5\dfrac{20}{36}$
$= 8\dfrac{26}{36} = 8\dfrac{13}{18}$

Press C 3 $a_{b/c}$ 1 $a_{b/c}$ 6 + 5 $a_{b/c}$ 5 $a_{b/c}$ 9 =

31. $8\dfrac{7}{15}$

$3\dfrac{2}{3} + 4\dfrac{4}{5} = 3\dfrac{10}{15} + 4\dfrac{12}{15}$
$= 7\dfrac{22}{15}$
$= 8\dfrac{7}{15}$

Press C 3 $a_{b/c}$ 2 $a_{b/c}$ 3 + 4 $a_{b/c}$ 4 $a_{b/c}$ 5 =

32. $12\frac{3}{28}$

$9\frac{6}{7} + 2\frac{1}{4} = 9\frac{24}{28} + 2\frac{7}{28}$

$\qquad = 11\frac{31}{28}$

$\qquad = 12\frac{3}{28}$

Press C 9 a_{b_c} 6 a_{b_c} 7 + 2 a_{b_c} 1 a_{b_c} 4 =

33. $4\frac{3}{10}$

$5\frac{3}{5} - 1\frac{3}{10} = 5\frac{6}{10} - 1\frac{3}{10}$

$\qquad = 4\frac{3}{10}$

34. $2\frac{7}{30}$

$4\frac{9}{10} - 2\frac{2}{3} = 4\frac{27}{30} - 2\frac{20}{30} = 2\frac{7}{30}$

35. $2\frac{17}{22}$

$6\frac{3}{11} - 3\frac{1}{2} = 6\frac{6}{22} - 3\frac{11}{22}$

$\qquad = 5\frac{28}{22} - 3\frac{11}{22}$

$\qquad = 2\frac{17}{22}$

Press C 6 a_{b_c} 3 a_{b_c} 1 1 − 3 a_{b_c} 1 a_{b_c} 2
=

36. $1\frac{1}{20}$

$2\frac{4}{5} - 1\frac{3}{4} = 2\frac{16}{20} - 1\frac{15}{20}$

$\qquad = 1\frac{1}{20}$

Press C 2 a_{b_c} 4 a_{b_c} 5 − 1 a_{b_c} 3 a_{b_c} 4 =

37. $\frac{17}{21}$

$4\frac{1}{7} - 3\frac{1}{3} = 4\frac{3}{21} - 3\frac{7}{21}$

$\qquad = 3\frac{24}{21} - 3\frac{7}{21}$

$\qquad = \frac{17}{21}$

Press C 4 a_{b_c} 1 a_{b_c} 7 − 3 a_{b_c} 1 a_{b_c} 3 =

38. $7\frac{7}{8}$

$12\frac{5}{8} - 4\frac{3}{4} = 12\frac{20}{32} - 4\frac{24}{32}$

$\qquad = 11\frac{52}{32} - 4\frac{24}{32}$

$\qquad = 7\frac{28}{32}$

$\qquad = 7\frac{7}{8}$

39.

$\qquad 3\frac{2}{5}$ mi. $\qquad 2\frac{1}{2}$ mi.

House $\qquad$ Library

$3\frac{2}{5} + 2\frac{1}{2} = 3\frac{4}{10} + 2\frac{5}{10} = 5\frac{9}{10}$

His house is **$5\frac{9}{10}$ mi.** away from the library.

40. $\frac{3}{5} + \frac{2}{7} = \frac{21}{35} + \frac{10}{35} = \frac{31}{35}$

$1 - \frac{31}{35} = \frac{4}{35}$

He had $\frac{4}{35}$ of his money left.

41. $3\frac{4}{9} - \frac{3}{5} = 3\frac{20}{45} - \frac{27}{45}$

$\qquad = 2\frac{65}{45} - \frac{27}{45}$

$\qquad = 2\frac{38}{45}$

Luke's rope was $2\frac{38}{45}$ yd.

$3\frac{4}{9} + 2\frac{38}{45} = 3\frac{20}{45} + 2\frac{38}{45}$

$\qquad = 5\frac{58}{45}$

$\qquad = 6\frac{13}{45}$

The total length of the rope brought by both of them was

$6\frac{13}{45}$ yd.

42. $1\frac{1}{4} + \frac{5}{6} = 1\frac{6}{24} + \frac{20}{24}$

$\qquad = 1\frac{26}{24}$

$\qquad = 2\frac{2}{24}$

$\qquad = 2\frac{1}{12}$

Clara took $2\frac{1}{12}$ hours to finish her English homework.

$1\frac{1}{4} + 2\frac{1}{12} = 1\frac{3}{12} + 2\frac{1}{12}$

$\qquad = 3\frac{4}{12}$

$\qquad = 3\frac{1}{3}$

Clara took **$3\frac{1}{3}$ hours** to finish all her homework.

43. $3\frac{3}{4} - 1\frac{7}{8} = 3\frac{6}{8} - 1\frac{7}{8}$

$\qquad = 2\frac{14}{8} - 1\frac{7}{8}$

$\qquad = 1\frac{7}{8}$

The mass of the papaya is $1\frac{7}{8}$ kg.

$3\frac{3}{4} + 1\frac{7}{8} = 3\frac{6}{8} + 1\frac{7}{8}$

$\qquad = 4\frac{13}{8}$

$\qquad = 5\frac{5}{8}$

The mass of the watermelon and the papaya is $5\frac{5}{8}$ kg.

$6\frac{1}{2} - 5\frac{5}{8} = 6\frac{4}{8} - 5\frac{5}{8}$

$\qquad = 5\frac{12}{8} - 5\frac{5}{8}$

$\qquad = \frac{7}{8}$

The mass of the honeydew is **$\frac{7}{8}$ kg.**

44. $5 - 3\frac{3}{4} = 4\frac{4}{4} - 3\frac{3}{4}$

$\qquad = 1\frac{1}{4}$

His sisters ate $1\frac{1}{4}$ pizzas.

106

$1\frac{1}{4} - \frac{7}{8} = 1\frac{2}{8} - \frac{7}{8}$

$\qquad\qquad = \frac{10}{8} - \frac{7}{8}$

$\qquad\qquad = \frac{3}{8}$

Terry ate $\frac{3}{8}$ pizzas.

$1\frac{1}{4} + \frac{3}{8} = 1\frac{2}{8} + \frac{3}{8} = 1\frac{5}{8}$

$1\frac{5}{8}$ pizzas were eaten in all.

45. $9 \div 4 = 2\frac{1}{4}$

$$4\overline{\smash{)}9} \quad \begin{array}{r} 2 \\ -8 \\ \hline 1 \end{array}$$

Her neighbour received **$2\frac{1}{4}$ litres** of syrup.

Unit 4: Fractions (Part 2)

1. $\frac{1}{6}$

$\frac{4}{9} \times \frac{3}{8} = \frac{4 \times 3}{9 \times 8} = \frac{12}{72} = \frac{1}{6}$

2. $\frac{5}{21}$

$\frac{5}{12} \times \frac{4}{7} = \frac{5 \times 4}{12 \times 7} = \frac{20}{84} = \frac{5}{21}$

3. $\frac{6}{25}$

$\frac{2}{5} \times \frac{6}{10} = \frac{2 \times 6}{5 \times 10} = \frac{12}{50} = \frac{6}{25}$

4. $\frac{11}{36}$

$\frac{11}{12}_4 \times \frac{\cancel{3}^1}{9} = \frac{11 \times 1}{4 \times 9} = \frac{11}{36}$

5. $\frac{2}{3}$

$\frac{\cancel{8}^2}{\cancel{9}_3} \times \frac{\cancel{3}^1}{\cancel{4}_1} = \frac{2}{3}$

6. $\frac{4}{15}$

$\frac{2}{5} \times \frac{2}{3} = \frac{2 \times 2}{5 \times 3} = \frac{4}{15}$

7. $1\frac{1}{35}$

$\frac{4}{7} \times \frac{9}{5} = \frac{4 \times 9}{7 \times 5} = \frac{36}{35} = 1\frac{1}{35}$

8. $3\frac{2}{11}$

Press $\boxed{C}\ \boxed{1}\ \boxed{0}\ \boxed{a_{b_c}}\ \boxed{1}\ \boxed{1}\ \boxed{\times}\ \boxed{2}\ \boxed{1}\ \boxed{a_{b_c}}\ \boxed{6}\ \boxed{=}$

9. $2\frac{13}{16}$

Press $\boxed{C}\ \boxed{3}\ \boxed{a_{b_c}}\ \boxed{8}\ \boxed{\times}\ \boxed{1}\ \boxed{5}\ \boxed{a_{b_c}}\ \boxed{2}\ \boxed{=}$

10. 1

$\frac{\cancel{18}^2}{\cancel{4}_2} \times \frac{\cancel{2}^1}{\cancel{9}_1} = \frac{2}{2} = 1$

11. $\frac{7}{24}$

$\frac{7}{3} \times \frac{1}{8} = \frac{7 \times 1}{3 \times 8} = \frac{7}{24}$

12. $3\frac{5}{6}$

Press $\boxed{C}\ \boxed{2}\ \boxed{3}\ \boxed{a_{b_c}}\ \boxed{5}\ \boxed{\times}\ \boxed{1}\ \boxed{0}\ \boxed{a_{b_c}}\ \boxed{1}\ \boxed{2}\ \boxed{=}$

13. $3\frac{1}{4}$

$\frac{13}{\cancel{10}_1} \times \frac{\cancel{20}^2}{8} = \frac{13 \times 2}{1 \times 8} = \frac{26}{8} = 3\frac{1}{4}$

14. 14

$\frac{\cancel{10}^2}{\cancel{3}_1} \times \frac{\cancel{21}^7}{\cancel{5}_1} = \frac{2 \times 7}{1 \times 1} = 14$

15. $23\frac{1}{3}$

Press $\boxed{C}\ \boxed{4}\ \boxed{9}\ \boxed{a_{b_c}}\ \boxed{9}\ \boxed{\times}\ \boxed{3}\ \boxed{0}\ \boxed{a_{b_c}}\ \boxed{7}\ \boxed{=}$

16. $9\frac{3}{4}$

$\frac{\cancel{9}^3}{2} \times \frac{13}{\cancel{6}_2} = \frac{3 \times 13}{2 \times 2} = \frac{39}{4} = 9\frac{3}{4}$

17. $3\frac{43}{44}$

Press $\boxed{C}\ \boxed{1}\ \boxed{5}\ \boxed{a_{b_c}}\ \boxed{1}\ \boxed{1}\ \boxed{\times}\ \boxed{3}\ \boxed{5}\ \boxed{a_{b_c}}\ \boxed{1}\ \boxed{2}\ \boxed{=}$

18. $24\frac{9}{56}$

Press $\boxed{C}\ \boxed{3}\ \boxed{3}\ \boxed{a_{b_c}}\ \boxed{8}\ \boxed{\times}\ \boxed{4}\ \boxed{1}\ \boxed{a_{b_c}}\ \boxed{7}\ \boxed{=}$

19. 104

$2\frac{3}{5} \times 40 = \frac{13}{\cancel{5}_1} \times \cancel{40}^8 = 13 \times 8 = 104$

20. $110\frac{1}{4}$

$6\frac{1}{8} \times 18 = \frac{49}{\cancel{8}_4} \times \cancel{18}^9 = \frac{49 \times 9}{4} = \frac{441}{4} = 110\frac{1}{4}$

21. 464

Press $\boxed{C}\ \boxed{8}\ \boxed{a_{b_c}}\ \boxed{2}\ \boxed{a_{b_c}}\ \boxed{7}\ \boxed{\times}\ \boxed{5}\ \boxed{6}\ \boxed{=}$

22. 558

Press $\boxed{C}\ \boxed{9}\ \boxed{9}\ \boxed{\times}\ \boxed{5}\ \boxed{a_{b_c}}\ \boxed{7}\ \boxed{a_{b_c}}\ \boxed{1}\ \boxed{1}\ \boxed{=}$

23. $53\frac{1}{3}$

$16 \times 3\frac{1}{3} = 16 \times \frac{10}{3} = \frac{16 \times 10}{3} = \frac{160}{3} = 53\frac{1}{3}$

24. $357\frac{2}{3}$

Press $\boxed{C}\ \boxed{7}\ \boxed{4}\ \boxed{\times}\ \boxed{4}\ \boxed{a_{b_c}}\ \boxed{5}\ \boxed{a_{b_c}}\ \boxed{6}\ \boxed{=}$

25. $\frac{1}{8}$

$\frac{3}{4} \div 6 = \frac{\cancel{3}^1}{4} \times \frac{1}{\cancel{6}_2} = \frac{1 \times 1}{4 \times 2} = \frac{1}{8}$

26. $\frac{1}{16}$

$\frac{5}{8} \div 10 = \frac{\cancel{5}^1}{8} \times \frac{1}{\cancel{10}_2} = \frac{1 \times 1}{8 \times 2} = \frac{1}{16}$

27. $\frac{2}{11}$

$\frac{4}{11} \div 2 = \frac{\cancel{4}^2}{11} \times \frac{1}{\cancel{2}_1} = \frac{2 \times 1}{11 \times 1} = \frac{2}{11}$

28. $\frac{1}{6}$

$\frac{6}{9} \div 4 = \frac{\cancel{6}^3}{9} \times \frac{1}{\cancel{4}_2} = \frac{3 \times 1}{9 \times 2} = \frac{3}{18} = \frac{1}{6}$

29. $\frac{1}{54}$

$\frac{2}{9} \div 12 = \frac{\cancel{2}^1}{9} \times \frac{1}{\cancel{12}_6} = \frac{1 \times 1}{9 \times 6} = \frac{1}{54}$

30. $\frac{1}{7}$

$\frac{6}{7} \div 6 = \frac{\cancel{6}^1}{7} \times \frac{1}{\cancel{6}_1} = \frac{1 \times 1}{7 \times 1} = \frac{1}{7}$

31. (a) $\dfrac{2}{\cancel{5}_1} \times \cancel{15}^3 = 6$

        $15 + 6 = 21$ oz.

        The total mass of the hazelnuts and cashews is **21 oz.**

    (b) $21 \div 8 = \dfrac{21}{8} = 2\dfrac{5}{8}$ oz.

        The mass of each package of mixed nuts is **$2\dfrac{5}{8}$ oz.**

32. $\dfrac{2}{9} \times \$4,815 = \$1,070$

    He saves $1,070.

    $\$4,815 - \$1,070 = \$3,745$

    $\dfrac{1}{2} \times \$3,745 = \$1,872.50$

    He spends **$1,872.50** on food.

33. $1 - \dfrac{3}{8} = \dfrac{5}{8}$

    $\dfrac{5}{8}$ of Jamal's money is $40 more than $\dfrac{5}{8}$ of Caroline's money.

    $\dfrac{5}{8} \rightarrow \$40$

    $\dfrac{1}{8} \rightarrow \$40 \div 5 = \$8$

    $\dfrac{8}{8} \rightarrow 8 \times \$8 = \$64$

    Jamal had **$64** more than Caroline in the beginning.

34.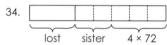

    lost   sister   4 × 72

    $4 \times 72 = 288$

    $(288 \div 3) \times 5 = 480$

    $(480 \div 2) \times 3 = 720$

    She had **720** marbles in the beginning.

35. Isaiah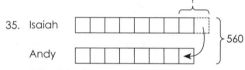

    Andy

    $560 \div 16 = 35$

    $2 \times 35 = 70$

    Isaiah had **70** more trading cards than Andy in the beginning.

36. $\dfrac{7}{12} \times 108 = 63$ m

    The width of Field A is 63 m.

    $(2 \times 63) + (2 \times 108) = 342$ m

    The perimeter of Field A is 342 m.

    $\dfrac{5}{6} \times 342 = 285$ m

    The perimeter of Field B is **285 m.**

37.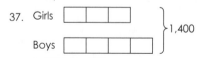

    Girls   Boys   1,400

    $1,400 \div 7 = 200$

    $3 \times 200 = 600$

    There are 600 girls in the school.

    $1,400 - 600 = 800$

    There are 800 boys in the school.

    $1 - \dfrac{1}{6} = \dfrac{5}{6}$

    $\dfrac{5}{6} \times 600 = 500$

    $1 - \dfrac{1}{5} = \dfrac{4}{5}$

    $\dfrac{4}{5} \times 800 = 640$

    $500 + 640 = 1,140$

1,140 students are in the other grade levels if $\dfrac{1}{6}$ of the girls and $\dfrac{1}{5}$ of the boys are in first grade.

38.

B	B	B	D	L	L	L

    B: Brother
    D: Drank
    L: Left

    She had $\dfrac{3}{7}$ of the orange juice left.

39. $\dfrac{5}{12} \times \$840 = \$350$

    $\dfrac{7}{10} \times \$350 = \$245$

    $\$245 \div 4 = \$61.25$

    Each dress cost **$61.25.**

40.

B	B	M	M	M		

    $756   B: Books   M: Mother

    $\$756 \div 3 = \$252$

    $9 \times \$252 = \$2,268$

    $\dfrac{3}{8} \rightarrow \$2,268$

    $\dfrac{1}{8} \rightarrow \$2,268 \div 3 = \$756$

    $\dfrac{8}{8} \rightarrow 8 \times \$756 = \$6,048$

    She had **$6,048** in her savings account in the beginning.

41. (a) $32 \times 45\dfrac{3}{4} = 1,464$ oz.

        The total mass of all 32 packages of red beans was **1,464 oz.**

    (b) $1 - \dfrac{1}{3} = \dfrac{2}{3}$

        $\dfrac{2}{3} \times 1,464 = 976$ oz.

        She had **976 oz.** of red beans left.

42.

Bl	Bl	M	B	B	B

    108   Bl: Blueberry   M: Multi-grain   B: Banana

    $6 \times 108 = 648$

    There were 648 blueberry, multi-grain, and banana muffins.

    $\dfrac{4}{7} \rightarrow 648$

    $\dfrac{1}{7} \rightarrow 648 \div 4 = 162$

    $\dfrac{3}{7} \rightarrow 3 \times 162 = 486$

    There were **486** carrot muffins.

Review 2

1. **(2)**

    $\dfrac{3}{8}$ is an unlike fraction.

2. **(2)**

    $\dfrac{1}{9} = 1 \div 9 \approx 0.111...$

    $21 + \dfrac{1}{9} \approx 21 + 0.11 = 21.11$

3. **(2)**

    $\dfrac{6}{11} \times \dfrac{2}{5} = \dfrac{6 \times 2}{11 \times 5} = \dfrac{12}{55}$

4. **(4)**

    $2\dfrac{4}{5} + 4\dfrac{2}{3} = 2\dfrac{12}{15} + 4\dfrac{10}{15} = 6\dfrac{22}{15} = 7\dfrac{7}{15}$

5. **(1)**

    $\dfrac{9}{10} \div 3 = \dfrac{\cancel{9}^3}{10} \times \dfrac{1}{\cancel{3}_1} = \dfrac{3}{10}$

6. **(1)**

$$\frac{4}{9} \div 12 = \frac{\cancel{4}^1}{9} \times \frac{1}{\cancel{12}_3} = \frac{1 \times 1}{9 \times 3} = \frac{1}{27}$$

7. **(4)**

$$\frac{1}{\cancel{4}_1} \times \frac{\cancel{12}^3}{8} = \frac{3}{8}$$

$$\frac{\cancel{8}^2}{\cancel{11}_1} \times \frac{\cancel{33}^3}{\cancel{4}_1} = 6$$

$$\frac{9}{\cancel{12}_4} \times \frac{\cancel{2}^1}{5} = \frac{9 \times 1}{4 \times 5} = \frac{9}{20}$$

$$\frac{\cancel{4}^1}{\cancel{11}_1} \times \frac{\cancel{33}^3}{\cancel{8}_2} = \frac{1 \times 3}{1 \times 2} = \frac{3}{2}$$

8. $\frac{3}{10}$ and $\frac{1}{10}$

9. **1,179**

   Press $\boxed{C}\ \boxed{1}\ \boxed{4}\ \boxed{a_{b_c}}\ \boxed{5}\ \boxed{a_{b_c}}\ \boxed{9}\ \boxed{\times}\ \boxed{8}\ \boxed{1}\ \boxed{=}$

10. $\mathbf{2\frac{1}{4}}$

    $9 \div 4 = \frac{9}{4} = 2\frac{1}{4}$

11. $\mathbf{3\frac{3}{5}}$

    $$\frac{\cancel{12}^6}{5} \times \frac{3}{\cancel{2}_1} = \frac{6 \times 3}{5 \times 1} = \frac{18}{5} = 3\frac{3}{5}$$

12. $\mathbf{\frac{1}{14}}$

    $$\frac{1}{2} - \frac{3}{7} = \frac{7}{14} - \frac{6}{14} = \frac{1}{14}$$

13. $\mathbf{\frac{3}{35}}$

    $$\frac{\cancel{2}^1}{7} \times \frac{3}{\cancel{10}_5} = \frac{1 \times 3}{7 \times 5} = \frac{3}{35}$$

14. **$59.45**

    $$\frac{1}{11} \times \$654 = \frac{654}{11} = 59\frac{5}{11}$$

    $59\frac{5}{11} \approx \$59 + \$0.454$

    $\phantom{59\frac{5}{11}} = \$59.454$

    $\phantom{59\frac{5}{11}} = \$59.45$

    $$\begin{array}{r} 0.454 \\ 11\overline{)5.0} \\ -44 \\ \hline 60 \\ -55 \\ \hline 50 \\ -44 \\ \hline 6 \end{array}$$

15. $\mathbf{3\frac{1}{4}}$

    $$8\frac{7}{12} - 5\frac{1}{3} = 8\frac{7}{12} - 5\frac{4}{12} = 3\frac{3}{12} = 3\frac{1}{4}$$

16.
    $$\overbrace{\begin{array}{|c|c|c|c|c|c|c|c|c|c|} \hline A & A & A & A & F & F & F & F & F & S \\ \hline \end{array}}^{10 \times 15}$$

    A: Animal
    F: Flower
    S: Scented

    $10 \times 15 = 150$

    $150 \div 10 = 15$

    There were **15** scented stickers.

17. $5\frac{1}{5} - 3\frac{1}{2} = 1\frac{7}{10}$ L

    The bottle holds $1\frac{7}{10}$ L of water.

    $5\frac{1}{5} + 1\frac{7}{10} = 6\frac{9}{10}$ L

    $$6\frac{9}{10} \div 30 = \frac{\cancel{69}^{23}}{10} \times \frac{1}{\cancel{30}_{10}} = \frac{23 \times 1}{10 \times 10} = \frac{23}{100}$$ L

    $$\frac{23}{100} \times 1,000 = 230 \text{ mL}$$

    Each glass contains **230 mL** of water.

18. $(7 \times 18) + 18 = 144$

    He gave away and sold 144 mangoes.

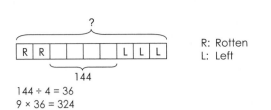

$144 \div 4 = 36$

$9 \times 36 = 324$

He had **324** mangoes in the beginning.

19.

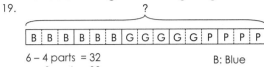

B: Blue
G: Green
P: Purple

$6 - 4 \text{ parts} = 32$

$ 2 \text{ parts} = 32$

$ 1 \text{ part} = 32 \div 2$

$\phantom{6 - 4 1 \text{ part}} = 16$

$ 15 \text{ parts} = 15 \times 16$

$\phantom{6 - 4 15 \text{ parts}} = 240$

Eduardo had **240** marbles in the beginning.

20.
    $$\overbrace{\begin{array}{|c|c|c|c|}\hline & 5 & & 5 \\ \hline \end{array}}^{?}$$
    $\underbrace{}_{125}$

    $\frac{2}{3}$ of the remaining apples = $5 + 125 = 130$

    $\frac{1}{3}$ of the remaining apples = $130 \div 2 = 65$

    $\frac{2}{3}$ of the apples at first = $(3 \times 65) + 5$

    $\phantom{\frac{2}{3} \text{ of the apples at first}} = 195 + 5$

    $\phantom{\frac{2}{3} \text{ of the apples at first}} = 200$

    $\frac{1}{3}$ of the apples at first = $200 \div 2 = 100$

    $3 \times 100 = 300$

    Mrs. Pappas had **300** apples in the beginning.

Unit 5: Area of Triangles

1. **AB; BC; CA**
   BC; 15 or **AB; 14**
   AB; 14 or **BC; 15**

2. **DE; EF; FD**
   DE; 6 or **EF; 12**
   EF; 12 or **DE; 6**

3. **XY; YZ; ZX**
   YZ; 4 or **XY; 9**
   XY; 9 or **YZ; 4**

4. Base = **4**
   Height = **7**
   Area = $\frac{1}{2} \times$ base $\times$ height
   $ = \frac{1}{2} \times 4 \times 7$
   $ = \mathbf{14}$

5. Base = **20**
   Height = **16**
   Area = $\frac{1}{2} \times$ base $\times$ height
   $ = \frac{1}{2} \times 20 \times 16$
   $ = \mathbf{160}$

6. Base = **8**
   Height = **37**
   Area = $\frac{1}{2} \times$ base $\times$ height
   $ = \frac{1}{2} \times 8 \times 37$
   $ = \mathbf{148}$

7. **72 cm²**

Area = $\frac{1}{2}$ × base × height

    = $\frac{1}{2}$ × 9 × 16

    = 72 cm²

8. **15 in.²**

Area = $\frac{1}{2}$ × base × height

    = $\frac{1}{2}$ × 3 × 10

    = 15 in.²

9. **76 cm²**

Area = $\frac{1}{2}$ × base × height

    = $\frac{1}{2}$ × 19 × 8

    = 76 cm²

10. **207 in.²**

Area = $\frac{1}{2}$ × base × height

    = $\frac{1}{2}$ × 23 × 18

    = 207 in.²

11. **60 cm²**

Area = $\frac{1}{2}$ × base × height

    = $\frac{1}{2}$ × 15 × 8

    = 60 cm²

12. **120 in.²**

Area = $\frac{1}{2}$ × base × height

    = $\frac{1}{2}$ × 30 × 8

    = 120 in.²

13. **80 cm²**

A = $\frac{1}{2}$ × base × height

    = $\frac{1}{2}$ × 10 × 10

    = 50 cm²

B = $\frac{1}{2}$ × base × height

    = $\frac{1}{2}$ × (10 − 2 − 2) × 10

    = $\frac{1}{2}$ × 6 × 10

    = 30 cm²

50 + 30 = 80 cm²

14. **302 in.²**

A = $\frac{1}{2}$ × base × height

    = $\frac{1}{2}$ × 18 × (28 − 10)

    = 162 in.²

B = $\frac{1}{2}$ × base × height

    = $\frac{1}{2}$ × (28 − 18) × 28

    = 140 in.²

162 + 140 = 302 in.²

15. **676 cm²**

$\left(\frac{1}{2} × 52 × 48\right) - \left(\frac{1}{2} × 52 × (48 − 26)\right)$

= 1248 − 572

= 676 cm²

16. **48 in.²**

$4 × \left(\frac{1}{2} × 4 × 6\right)$ = 48 in.²

17. **108 cm²**

$\frac{1}{2}$ × 24 × 18 = 216 cm²

216 ÷ 2 = 108 cm²

18. **330.5 in.²**

$2 × \left(\frac{1}{2} × 16 × 20\right) + \left(\frac{1}{2} × 7 × 3\right)$

= 320 + 10.5

= 330.5 in.²

19. **128 cm²**

$4 × \left(\frac{1}{2} × 8 × 8\right)$ = 128 cm²

20. **40 in.²**

20 ÷ 5 = 4 in.

$5 × \left(\frac{1}{2} × 4 × 4\right)$ = 40 in.²

Unit 6: Ratio

1. **6 : 5**
   5 : 6

2. **8 : 3**
   3 : 8

3. **5 : 3**
   3 : 5

chickens : ducks	ducks : chickens
15 : 9	9 : 15
5 : 3	3 : 5

4. **2 : 3**
   3 : 2

Stick A : Stick B	Stick B : Stick A
30 : 45	45 : 30
2 : 3	3 : 2

5. **2 : 1**
   1 : 2

watermelon : papaya	papaya : watermelon
4 : 2	2 : 4
2 : 1	1 : 2

6. (a) **13 : 12**
   12 : 13

Perimeter of Rectangle A = (8 × 2) + (5 × 2)

    = 26 in.

Perimeter of Rectangle B = (4 × 2) + (8 × 2)

    = 24 in.

A : B → ÷2 (26 : 24) ÷2 → 13 : 12

B : A → ÷2 (24 : 26) ÷2 → 12 : 13

(b) **5 : 4**
   4 : 5

Area of Rectangle A = 8 × 5 = 40 in.²

Area of Rectangle B = 4 × 8 = 32 in.²

A : B → ÷8 (40 : 32) ÷8 → 5 : 4

B : A → ÷8 (32 : 40) ÷8 → 4 : 5

7. **7 : 9**

÷3 (21 : 27) ÷3 → 7 : 9

8. **2 : 7**

÷9 (18 : 63) ÷9 → 2 : 7

Singapore Math Practice Level 5A

9. **8 : 7**
$$\div 8 \begin{pmatrix} 64 : 56 \\ 8 : 7 \end{pmatrix} \div 8$$

10. **5 : 24**
$$\div 5 \begin{pmatrix} 25 : 120 \\ 5 : 24 \end{pmatrix} \div 5$$

11. **7 : 5**
$$\div 12 \begin{pmatrix} 84 : 60 \\ 7 : 5 \end{pmatrix} \div 12$$

12. **9 : 5 : 6**
$$\begin{pmatrix} 90 \\ 9 \end{pmatrix} \div 10 : \begin{pmatrix} 50 \\ 5 \end{pmatrix} \div 10 : \begin{pmatrix} 60 \\ 6 \end{pmatrix} \div 10$$

13. **2 : 3 : 6**
$$\begin{pmatrix} 36 \\ 2 \end{pmatrix} \div 18 : \begin{pmatrix} 54 \\ 3 \end{pmatrix} \div 18 : \begin{pmatrix} 108 \\ 6 \end{pmatrix} \div 18$$

14. **9 : 19 : 14**
$$\begin{pmatrix} 45 \\ 9 \end{pmatrix} \div 5 : \begin{pmatrix} 95 \\ 19 \end{pmatrix} \div 5 : \begin{pmatrix} 70 \\ 14 \end{pmatrix} \div 5$$

15. **7 : 6 : 5**
$$\begin{pmatrix} 91 \\ 7 \end{pmatrix} \div 13 : \begin{pmatrix} 78 \\ 6 \end{pmatrix} \div 13 : \begin{pmatrix} 65 \\ 5 \end{pmatrix} \div 13$$

16. **4 : 3 : 9**
$$\begin{pmatrix} 100 \\ 4 \end{pmatrix} \div 25 : \begin{pmatrix} 75 \\ 3 \end{pmatrix} \div 25 : \begin{pmatrix} 225 \\ 9 \end{pmatrix} \div 25$$

17. **25**
$$\times 5 \begin{pmatrix} 8 : 5 \\ 40 : 25 \end{pmatrix} \times 5$$

18. **21**
$$\times 3 \begin{pmatrix} 6 : 7 \\ 18 : 21 \end{pmatrix} \times 3$$

19. **8**
$$\div 12 \begin{pmatrix} 108 : 96 \\ 9 : 8 \end{pmatrix} \div 12$$

20. **36**
$$\times 6 \begin{pmatrix} 9 : 6 \\ 54 : 36 \end{pmatrix} \times 6$$

21. **7**
$$\div 11 \begin{pmatrix} 77 : 88 \\ 7 : 8 \end{pmatrix} \div 11$$

22. **32; 12**
$$\begin{pmatrix} 8 \\ 32 \end{pmatrix} \times 4 : \begin{pmatrix} 6 \\ 24 \end{pmatrix} \times 4 : \begin{pmatrix} 3 \\ 12 \end{pmatrix} \times 4$$

23. **63; 36**
$$\begin{pmatrix} 3 \\ 27 \end{pmatrix} \times 9 : \begin{pmatrix} 7 \\ 63 \end{pmatrix} \times 9 : \begin{pmatrix} 4 \\ 36 \end{pmatrix} \times 9$$

24. **10; 25**
$$\begin{pmatrix} 2 \\ 10 \end{pmatrix} \times 5 : \begin{pmatrix} 9 \\ 45 \end{pmatrix} \times 5 : \begin{pmatrix} 5 \\ 25 \end{pmatrix} \times 5$$

25. **5; 8**
$$\begin{pmatrix} 60 \\ 5 \end{pmatrix} \div 12 : \begin{pmatrix} 96 \\ 8 \end{pmatrix} \div 12 : \begin{pmatrix} 36 \\ 3 \end{pmatrix} \div 12$$

26. **9; 7**
$$\begin{pmatrix} 72 \\ 9 \end{pmatrix} \div 8 : \begin{pmatrix} 48 \\ 6 \end{pmatrix} \div 8 : \begin{pmatrix} 56 \\ 7 \end{pmatrix} \div 8$$

27. (a) **13 : 21**
boys : all students
$$\div 2 \begin{pmatrix} 26 : 42 \\ 13 : 21 \end{pmatrix} \div 2$$

(b) **8 : 13**
42 − 26 = 16
There are 16 girls on the school bus.

girls : boys
$$\div 2 \begin{pmatrix} 16 : 26 \\ 8 : 13 \end{pmatrix} \div 2$$

28. **1 : 3**
46 ÷ 2 = 23
There are 23 comic books on the shelf.
46 + 23 = 69
There are a total of 69 books on the shelf.
comic books : total books
$$\div 23 \begin{pmatrix} 23 : 69 \\ 1 : 3 \end{pmatrix} \div 23$$

29. **5 : 13**
15 + 24 = 39
The distance from Town A to Town B is 39 mi.
$$\div 3 \begin{pmatrix} 15 : 39 \\ 5 : 13 \end{pmatrix} \div 3$$

30. (a) **16 : 29**
postcard : letter
$$\div 5 \begin{pmatrix} 80 : 145 \\ 16 : 29 \end{pmatrix} \div 5$$

(b) **5 : 9**
200-g package : 300-g package
$$\div 100 \begin{pmatrix} 500 : 900 \\ 5 : 9 \end{pmatrix} \div 100$$

(c) **4 : 15**
3 × $0.80 = $2.40
The postage for 3 postcards is $2.40.
postcards : package
$$\div 60 \begin{pmatrix} 240 : 900 \\ 4 : 15 \end{pmatrix} \div 60$$

31. **3 : 6 : 5**
triangles : squares : crosses
3 : 6 : 5

32. **2 : 3 : 9**
A : C : total
2 : 3 : (2 + 4 + 3)
2 : 3 : 9

33. **14 : 19 : 8**
senior citizen : adult : child
$$\begin{pmatrix} 42 \\ 14 \end{pmatrix} \div 3 : \begin{pmatrix} 57 \\ 19 \end{pmatrix} \div 3 : \begin{pmatrix} 24 \\ 8 \end{pmatrix} \div 3$$

34. **2 : 1**
longest : shortest
$$\div 8 \begin{pmatrix} 16 : 8 \\ 2 : 1 \end{pmatrix} \div 8$$

35. adults : children
$$\times 17 \begin{pmatrix} 5 : 6 \\ 85 : 102 \end{pmatrix} \times 17$$
85 + 102 = 187
There are **187** people in the library.

36. (8 − 3) parts = 245
5 parts = 245
1 part = 245 ÷ 5 = 49
8 parts = 8 × 49 = 392
392 boots are in the store.

37. weekday : weekend
$$\times 14 \begin{pmatrix} 3 : 4 \\ 42 : 56 \end{pmatrix} \times 14$$
2 × $56 = $112
She earns **$112** for working on Saturday and Sunday.

38. (a) roses : all flowers
22 : 22 + 12 + 16
$$\div 2 \begin{pmatrix} 22 : 50 \\ 11 : 25 \end{pmatrix} \div 2$$

Singapore Math Practice Level 5A

The ratio of roses to the total number of flowers in the bouquet is **11 : 25**.

(b) daisies : carnations

$$\times 12 \left(\begin{array}{c} 1 : 3 \\ 12 : 36 \end{array} \right) \times 12$$

36 – 16 = 20

20 carnations must be added to the bouquet so that the ratio of daisies to carnations becomes 1 : 3.

39. $\frac{3}{7} \times 3,500 = 1,500$ g

1,500 g of flour are used for baking the tarts.
3,500 – 1,500 – 700 = 1,300 g

cake	: tarts	: remaining flour
700 ÷ 100	: 1,500 ÷ 100	: 1,300 ÷ 100
7	: 15	: 13

The ratio of flour used for baking the cake to flour used for baking the tarts to the remaining flour is **7 : 15 : 13**.

40. (a) Peter   : Anya   : Oliver

$$\begin{array}{ccc} 2 & : 5 & : 4 \\ 72 & : 180 & : 144 \end{array} \times 36$$

$72 + $180 + $144 = $396

The sum of money is **$396**.

(b)

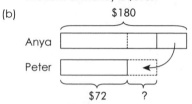

$180 – $72 = $108
$108 ÷ 2 = $54

Anya must give **$54** to Peter so that they both will get an equal share.

41. Trina : Madison : Li

$$\begin{array}{ccc} 7 & : 6 & \\ & 3_{\times 2} & : 5_{\times 2} \\ 7 & : 6 & : 10 \end{array}$$

Li   : total stamps
10   : 7 + 6 + 10
10   : 23

The ratio of stamps that Li has to the total number of stamps the 3 girls have is **10 : 23**.

42. $64 ÷ 2 = $32

The cost of each adult train ticket is $32.

adult : child

$$\times 4 \left(\begin{array}{c} 8 : 5 \\ 32 : 20 \end{array} \right) \times 4$$

The cost of a child's train ticket is **$20**.

Review 3

1. **(4)**

$$\times 3 \left(\begin{array}{c} 5 : 7 \\ 15 : 21 \end{array} \right) \times 3$$

2. **(3)**

46 – 18 = 28

bills : coins

$$\div 2 \left(\begin{array}{c} 28 : 18 \\ 14 : 9 \end{array} \right) \div 2$$

3. **(1)**

Molly : Hilda

$$\times 8 \left(\begin{array}{c} 4 : 9 \\ 32 : 72 \end{array} \right) \times 8$$

4. **(2)**

Area of rectangle = 30 × 20
= 600 in.²

Area of the largest triangle = $\frac{1}{2}$ × 30 × 20
= 300 in.²

Area of the other unshaded triangle = $\frac{1}{2}$ × 15 × 20
= 150 in.²

Area of shaded triangle = 600 – 300 – 150
= 150 in.²

5. **(2)**

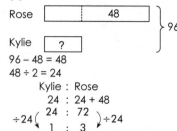

96 – 48 = 48
48 ÷ 2 = 24

Kylie : Rose
24 : 24 + 48

$$\div 24 \left(\begin{array}{c} 24 : 72 \\ 1 : 3 \end{array} \right) \div 24$$

6. **(2)**

3 years 6 months – 1 year = 2 years 6 months

Penny : Henry
3 yr. 6 mo. : 2 yr. 6 mo.

$$\div 6 \left(\begin{array}{c} 42 : 30 \\ 7 : 5 \end{array} \right) \div 6$$

7. **(2)**

$\frac{1}{2}$ × base × height = $\frac{1}{2}$ × 24 × 12 = 144 cm²

8. **5 : 14 : 12**

$$\begin{array}{ccc} 15 ÷ 3 & : 42 ÷ 3 & : 36 ÷ 3 \\ 5 & : 14 & : 12 \end{array}$$

9. **600 students**

3 + 20 parts = 690
1 part = 690 ÷ 23
= 30
20 parts = 20 × 30
= 600

10. **4 : 7**

girls : children
24 : 18 + 24

$$\div 6 \left(\begin{array}{c} 24 : 42 \\ 4 : 7 \end{array} \right) \div 6$$

11. **164 in.**

3 + 4 parts = 287 in.
1 part = 287 ÷ 7
= 41 in.
4 parts = 4 × 41
= 164 in.

12. **6 : 9 : 11**

squares : triangles : circles
6 : 9 : 11

13. **7,536 nonfiction books**

fiction : nonfiction

$$\times 2,512 \left(\begin{array}{c} 5 : 3 \\ 12,560 : 7,536 \end{array} \right) \times 2,512$$

14. **13 cm²**

$\frac{1}{2}$ × base × height = $\frac{1}{2}$ × 2 × 13
= 13 cm²

15. **55 in.²**

$\frac{1}{2}$ × base × height = $\frac{1}{2}$ × (45 – 40) × 22
= 55 in.²

Singapore Math Practice Level 5A

16. $96 \div 4 = 24$ cm
    Each side of the square is 24 cm.

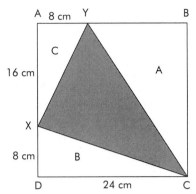

Area of square ABCD = $24 \times 24 = 576$ cm²

Area of triangle A = $\frac{1}{2} \times (24 - 8) \times (16 + 8)$
$= 192$ cm²

Area of triangle B = $\frac{1}{2} \times 24 \times 8$
$= 96$ cm²

Area of triangle C = $\frac{1}{2} \times 8 \times 16$
$= 64$ cm²

Area of shaded triangle = $576 - 192 - 96 - 64$
$= 224$ cm²

The area of the shaded triangle is **224 cm²**.

17. $(5 + 3 + 2)$ parts = 970
    1 part = $970 \div 10$
    $= 97$
    $5 - 2$ parts = 3×97
    3 parts = 291
    There were **291** fewer German tourists than Japanese tourists.

18. $\times 36 \big(\begin{array}{ccc} 5 & : & 7 \\ 180 & : & 252 \end{array} \big) \times 36$

    $180 \div 4 = 45$
    The length of the smaller square is **45 cm**.

19. Base of each triangle = $28 \div 2 = 14$ cm
    Height of each triangle = $20 \div 2 = 10$ cm

    $\frac{1}{2} \times$ base $\times$ height $= \frac{1}{2} \times 14 \times 10 = 70$

    The area of each triangle is **70 cm²**.

20.   footballs : basketballs
    $\times 4 \big(\begin{array}{ccc} 3 & : & 5 \\ 12 & : & 10 \end{array} \big) \times 2$
    $(12 - 3) + (10 - 5)$ parts = 406
    $9 + 5$ parts = 406
    1 part = $406 \div 14 = 29$
    $(12 + 10)$ parts = $22 \times 29 = 638$
    The total number of footballs and basketballs in the store is now **638**.

Final Review

1. **(1)**

Millions	Hundred Thousands	Ten Thousands	Thousands	Hundreds	Tens	Ones
9	4	0	3	5	1	2

2. **(3)**

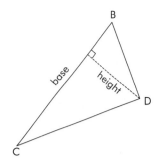

3. **(1)**
   Area = $\frac{1}{2} \times$ base $\times$ height
   $= \frac{1}{2} \times 4 \times 2$
   $= 4$ in.²

4. **(1)**
   $9,859 \div 9 \approx 10,000 \div 10 = 1,000$

5. **(2)**
   Tamika : both girls
   $36 : 36 + 54$
   $\div 18 \big(\begin{array}{ccc} 36 & : & 90 \\ 2 & : & 5 \end{array} \big) \div 18$

6. **(3)**
   $53,625 - 51,125 = 2,500$
   $61,125 - 58,625 = 2,500$
   $53,625 + 2,500 = 56,125$

7. **(2)**
   $\begin{array}{r} {}^{1}\,{}^{3}_{2}\,{}^{4}1\,2\,5 \\ \times \quad\quad 6\,9 \\ \hline 1,1\,2\,5 \\ +\ 7\,5\,0 \\ \hline 8,6\,2\,5 \end{array}$

8. **(4)**
   $4,938 + 6,054 = 10,992$
   $10,992 + 19,835 = 30,827$

9. **(3)**
   $8\frac{4}{5}$ of 30 = $8\frac{4}{5} \times 30$
   $= \frac{44}{\cancel{5}_1} \times \cancel{30}^6$
   $= 264$

10. **(3)**
    9,090,909

11. **(3)**
    Area of triangle DAB = $\frac{1}{2} \times$ base $\times$ height
    $= \frac{1}{2} \times 12 \times 12$
    $= 72$ in.²

12. **(1)**
    $\$10 = 10 \times 100 = 1,000¢$
    $\div 250 \big(\begin{array}{ccc} 250 & : & 1,000 \\ 1 & : & 4 \end{array} \big) \div 250$

13. **(3)**
    $7\frac{5}{7} = 7 + \frac{5}{7}$
    $\approx 7 + 0.714$
    $= 7.71$ (2 decimal places)

    $\begin{array}{r} 0.7\,1\,4 \\ 7\overline{)5.0} \\ -4\,9 \\ \hline 1\,0 \\ -\ 7 \\ \hline 3\,0 \\ -2\,8 \\ \hline 2 \end{array}$

14. **(3)**
    $12\frac{1}{5} - 5\frac{1}{10} = 12\frac{2}{10} - 5\frac{1}{10}$
    $= 7\frac{1}{10}$

15. **(4)**
$6,384 ÷ $21 = 304
304 × 2 = 608

16. **196 000**
195,643 ≈ 196,000

17. **seventy thousand**

Millions	Thousands	Ten Thousands	Thousands	Hundreds	Tens	Ones
1	0	7	3	5	6	4

18. **492 cm²**
$\frac{1}{2} × 41 × 24 = 492$ cm²

19. **4 : 17**

  fail : pass
  8 : (42 − 8)
  ÷2 (8 : 34) ÷2
  4 : 17

20. **1,160 in.²**
$\frac{1}{2} ×$ base × height $= \frac{1}{2} × (32 + 8) × 58$

$= \frac{1}{2} × 40 × 58$

$= 1,160$ in.²

21. **$2,016**
12 × 84 = 1,008
1,008 × $2 = $2,016

22. **15 cm²**
$\frac{1}{2} ×$ base × height $= \frac{1}{2} × 5 × 6$

$= 15$ cm²

23. **57**
$4\frac{6}{8} × 12 = \frac{38}{8_2} × 12^3 = \frac{114}{2} = 57$

24. **3,509,000**

25. **1.25 L**
3,750 + 8,750 = 12,500 mL
12,500 ÷ 10 = 1,250 mL
1,250 ÷ 1,000 = 1.25 L

26. **10**

  18) ÷3 : 30) ÷3 : 72) ÷3
  6   : 10   : 24

27. **$\frac{6}{11}$**
$1 − \frac{3}{11} = \frac{8}{11}$

$\frac{1}{4} × \frac{8}{11} = \frac{2}{11}$

$1 − \left(\frac{3}{11} + \frac{2}{11}\right) = \frac{6}{11}$

28. **750 g**
$1 − \frac{3}{4} = \frac{1}{4}$

$\frac{1}{4} × 3,000 = 750$ g

29. **1 : 5**

  Derrick : his father
  8 : 32 + 8
  ÷8 (8 : 40) ÷8
  1 : 5

30. **6,992**
80 × (69 + 22) − 288 = 80 × 91 − 288
$= 6,992$

31. **237**
Press C 7 5 × 3 + 1 0 8 ÷ (2 7 ÷ 3) =

32. **81,614**
Press C 9 4 9 × 8 6

33. **$10\frac{19}{45}$**
Press C 3 6 aʙⅽ 5 + 2 9 aʙⅽ 9 =

34. **98**
Press C 3 5 2 8 ÷ 3 6 =

35. **$\frac{3}{28}$**
Press C 3 aʙⅽ 4 ÷ 7 =

36.
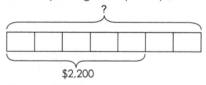

$35.50 − $31.50 = $4
Each cup costs $4.
$35.50 − (4 × $4) = $19.50
The cost of 3 plates is $19.50.
3 × $19.50 = $58.50
The cost of 9 plates is **$58.50.**

37. $\frac{1}{2} ×$ base × height $= \frac{1}{2} × 5 × 8 = 20$ cm²
The area of each triangle is 20 cm².
8 × 20 = 160
The area of the octagon is **160 cm².**

38. $2\frac{1}{2} × $880 = \frac{5}{2} × $880 = $2,200$
The tour package to Japan is $2,200.

  [bar model: ? over 7 parts, $2,200 under 5 parts]

5 parts = $2,200
 1 part = $2,200 ÷ 5 = $440
7 parts = 7 × $440 = $3,080
The tour package to England is $3,080.

$880 + $2,200 + $3,080 = $6,160
The total cost of all 3 tour packages is **$6,160.**

39. $6\frac{1}{4} + 2\frac{7}{8} = 9\frac{1}{8}$
The mass of Basket B is $9\frac{1}{8}$ lb.

$21\frac{3}{5} − 6\frac{1}{4} − 9\frac{1}{8} = 6\frac{9}{40}$
The mass of Basket C is $6\frac{9}{40}$ lb.

$6\frac{1}{4} = 6\frac{10}{40}$
The mass of Basket A is $6\frac{10}{40}$ lb.

$9\frac{1}{8} − 6\frac{9}{40} = 2\frac{9}{10}$
The difference between the mass of the heaviest and the lightest baskets of vegetables is **$2\frac{9}{10}$ lb.**

40. 112 ÷ 4 = 28
The side of the smaller square is 28 cm.

Singapore Math Practice Level 5A

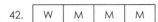

28 × 28 = 784
The area of the smaller square is 784 cm².
36 × 36 = 1,296
The area of the bigger square is 1,296 cm².
1,296 − 784 = 512
The difference in the area of the 2 squares is **512 cm²**.

41. Common factors of 3 and 4 = 12, 24, 36, 48, 60

12 spoons, 12 forks → (12 ÷ 4) × $3 − (12 ÷ 3) × $2
                                  = $1 of difference

60 spoons, 60 forks → (60 ÷ 4) × $3 − (60 ÷ 3) × $2
                                  = $5 of difference

(60 ÷ 4) × $3 + (60 ÷ 3) × $2 = $45 + $40
                                  = $85
She spent **$85** altogether.

42.

W	M	M	M

After 56 women joined the health club,

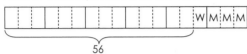

56

14 parts = 56
  1 part = 56 ÷ 14 = 4
  3 parts = 3 × 4 = 12
There were **12** men in the health club.

43.

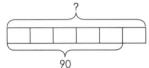

90

5 parts = 90
  1 part = 90 ÷ 5 = 18
  6 parts = 6 × 18 = 108

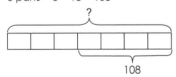

108

4 parts = 108
  1 part = 108 ÷ 4 = 27
  7 parts = 7 × 27 = 189
There were **189** pieces of paper in the beginning.

44. Anton : Michael : Paloma
              12   : 11
  3₍×3₎ : 4₍×3₎
  9   :   12   : 11
(9 + 12 + 11) parts = 224
            1 part = 224 ÷ 32
                   = 7
      (11 − 9) parts = 2 × 7
                   = 14
The difference between Paloma's and Anton's points on the
English test is **14**.

45. 50 × $34 = $1,700
He would earn $1,700 if he sold all 50 watches.
$1,700 − $986 = $714
He earned $714 less.
$68 + $34 = $102
He had a loss of $102 for every unsold watch.
$714 ÷ $102 = 7
7 watches were not sold that month.

46.

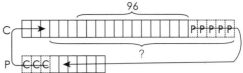

12 parts = 96
  1 part = 96 ÷ 12
         = 8
20 parts = 20 × 8
         = 160
She had **160** trading cards in the beginning.

47. (a) 5 parts = 60 + 5
              = 65
      1 part = 65 ÷ 5
              = 13
    13 − 5 = 8
    Julia was 8 years old 5 years ago.
      Julia : Grandmother
    ÷4 (8 : 60) ÷4
         2 : 15
    The ratio of Julia's age 5 years ago to her grandmother's
    age 5 years ago is **2 : 15**.

  (b) $\frac{2}{5}$ × 65 = 26
    26 − 13 = 13
    Julia's age will be $\frac{2}{5}$ of her grandmother's present age in
    13 years.

48. 3 parts = $6 + $36 = $42
  1 part = $42 ÷ 3
         = $14
7 × $14 = $98
Aaron had **$98** in the beginning.
4 × $14 = $56
David had **$56** in the beginning.

Calculator Skills

1. **9,372**
    Press C 8 5 2 × 1 1 =

2. **612,297**
    Press C 9 7 1 9 × 6 3 =

3. **35**
    Press C 4 2 0 ÷ 1 2 =

4. **294**
    Press C 6 7 6 2 ÷ 2 3 =

5. **75**
    Press C 7 1 + 1 3 − 9 =

6. **578**
    Press C 5 6 2 + 1 1 2 ÷ 7 =

7. **1,325**
    Press C 2 5 × (3 5 + 1 8) =

8. **10**
    Press C 3 6 0 0 ÷ (9 8 2 − 6 2 2) =

9. **8,484**
    Press C (1 4 9 − 1 2 6 + 7 8) × 4 2 0 ÷ 5 =

10. **4,888**
Press C 6 9 7 8 − 1 5 × (2 2 × 1 9 ÷ 3) =

11. **0.44**
Press C 4 ÷ 9 =

12. **0.55**
Press C 6 ÷ 1 1 =

13. **0.13**
Press C 1 ÷ 8 =

14. **7.11**
Press C 1 ÷ 9 + 7 =

15. **13.73**
Press C 8 ÷ 1 1 + 1 3 =

16. $14\frac{3}{4}$
Press C 5 a_{b_c} 1 a_{b_c} 2 + 9 a_{b_c} 1 a_{b_c} 4 =

17. $36\frac{7}{24}$
Press C 2 2 a_{b_c} 1 a_{b_c} 6 + 1 4 a_{b_c} 1 a_{b_c} 8 =

18. $109\frac{68}{77}$
Press C 4 9 a_{b_c} 3 a_{b_c} 7 + 6 0 a_{b_c} 5 a_{b_c} 1 1 =

19. $44\frac{2}{15}$
Press C 7 8 a_{b_c} 5 a_{b_c} 6 − 3 4 a_{b_c} 7 a_{b_c} 1 0 =

20. $45\frac{1}{36}$
Press C 5 3 a_{b_c} 1 a_{b_c} 4 − 8 a_{b_c} 2 a_{b_c} 9 =

21. $1\frac{11}{24}$
Press C 1 4 a_{b_c} 8 × 5 a_{b_c} 6 =

22. $7\frac{4}{5}$
Press C 2 6 a_{b_c} 5 × 3 a_{b_c} 2 =

23. $39\frac{1}{9}$
Press C 8 8 a_{b_c} 1 2 × 1 6 a_{b_c} 3 =

24. $2\frac{4}{5}$
Press C 2 1 a_{b_c} 5 × 2 a_{b_c} 3 =

25. **88**
Press C 1 a_{b_c} 3 a_{b_c} 8 × 6 4 =

26. $484\frac{1}{2}$
Press C 5 a_{b_c} 1 a_{b_c} 1 0 × 9 5 =

27. $1,733\frac{1}{3}$
Press C 1 0 4 × 1 6 a_{b_c} 2 a_{b_c} 3 =

28. $144\frac{2}{3}$
Press C 2 1 × 6 a_{b_c} 8 a_{b_c} 9 =

29. $\frac{1}{32}$
Press C 1 a_{b_c} 4 ÷ 8 =

30. $\frac{1}{24}$
Press C 5 a_{b_c} 1 2 ÷ 1 0 =

31. $\frac{3}{10}$
Press C 9 a_{b_c} 1 0 ÷ 3 =

32. $\frac{3}{11}$
Press C 6 a_{b_c} 1 1 ÷ 2 =

33. $\frac{1}{18}$
Press C 7 a_{b_c} 9 ÷ 1 4 =

34. $\frac{1}{32}$
Press C 3 a_{b_c} 4 ÷ 2 4 =

35. $\frac{1}{15}$
Press C 2 a_{b_c} 5 ÷ 6 =

Challenge Questions

1. $1,234 \times 789 = 973,626$
$2,345 \times 678 = 1,589,910$
$3,456 \times 567 = 1,959,552$

1,234	973,626	789
2,345	**1,589,910**	678
3,456	**1,959,552**	567

2. Using the Guess and Check method,
Guess 1:

  2   7   0 __ __ __ __

0 is not an even number, so Guess 1 is eliminated.
Guess 2:

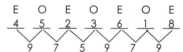

Guess 2 fits all conditions, so the answer is **4,523,618**.

3. *Possible answer:*
Step 1: Cut the orange in half (1st cut).
Step 2: Stack the 2 halves.
Step 3: Cut the oranges in half (2nd cut).

4. Kofi : Marcus : Andy
 1 × 5 : 2 × 5
          5 × 2 : 7 × 2
  5 :   10   : 14
14 − 10 parts = 144
    1 part = 144 ÷ 4 = 36
 14 − 5 parts = 9 × 36
    9 parts = 324
The difference between the stamps collected by Kofi and Andy is **324**.

Singapore Math Practice Level 5A

5. $6 + 2 = 8$
   $10 + 18 = 28$
   $120 - 46 = 74$

6	2	8
10	18	28
46	**74**	120

6.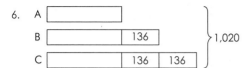

   $1,020 - (3 \times 136) = 612$
   $612 \div 3 = 204$
   There are 204 coins in Container A.

   $204 + 136 = 340$
   There are 340 coins in Container B.

   $340 + 136 = 476$
   There are 476 coins in Container C.

   $$A : B : C$$
   $$204 : 340 : 476$$
   $$3 : 5 : 7$$

   The ratio of coins in Container A to coins in Container B to coins in Container C is **3 : 5 : 7**.

7. $y = \frac{2}{3} \times 6 = 4$ cm
   base of each small triangle $= 10 \div 2$
   $ = 5$ cm
   Area of each unshaded triangle
   $= \frac{1}{2} \times$ base $\times$ height
   $= \frac{1}{2} \times 4 \times 5$
   $= 10$ cm²
   The area of each unshaded triangle is **10 cm²**.

8. last digit $= 5$
   third digit $= 1\frac{3}{5} \times 5 = 8$
   second digit $= \frac{3}{4} \times 8 = 6$
   first digit $= \frac{2}{3} \times 6 = 4$
   Keiko earns **$4,685**.

9. <u>Possible values of M when it is divided by 4:</u>
   63, 67, 71, 75, 79, (83), 87
   <u>Possible values of M when it is divided by 5:</u>
   68, 73, 78, (83), 88
   $83 \div 4 = 20$ R 3
   $83 \div 5 = 16$ R 3
   M is **83**.

10. $y = \frac{3}{4} \times 8 = 6$ in.
    base $= 1\frac{3}{4} \times 8 = 14$ in.
    shaded area $= (\frac{1}{2} \times 14 \times 8) - (\frac{1}{2} \times 14 \times 6)$
    $ = 56 - 42$
    $ = 14$ cm²
    The shaded area is **14 in.²**.

11.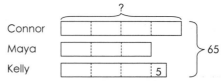

    $65 - 5 = 60$
    $60 \div 10 = 6$
    $4 \times 6 = 24$
    Kelvin is the oldest among the 3 of them.
    The age of the oldest person is **24 years old**.

12. first : second   third : last   first : last
       3 : 1   1 : 3   2 : 3
    Multiply the ratio of the first digit to the last digit by 3.
             first : last
             $2_{\times 3} : 3_{\times 3}$
              6 : 9
    Multiply the ratio of the first digit to the second digit by 2.
           first : second
           $3_{\times 2} : 1_{\times 2}$
            6 : 2
    Multiply the ratio of the third digit to the last digit by 3.
            third : last
            $1_{\times 3} : 3_{\times 3}$
            3 : 9
    $6 + 2 + 3 + 9 = 20$
    I am **6,239**.

Notes

Notes

119

Notes

Notes

Singapore Math Practice Level 5A

Notes

Notes

Singapore Math Practice Level 5A

Notes

Notes

Notes

Singapore Math Practice Level 5A

Notes

Singapore Math Practice Level 5A

Notes